# Half in Islam, Whole in Jesus

## A WOMAN'S WORTH

**Mona Sabah**

GETHSEMANE PRESS

GETHSEMANE PRESS
Half in Islam, Whole in Jesus - A Woman's Worth
Copyright © 2019 by Mona Sabah

This title is also available as an eBook
ISBN-13: 978-0-9986378-2-2 (soft cover)

Library of Congress Control Number: [LCCN]: 2019910976
Published by GETHSEMANE PRESS
Edmond, Oklahoma

Scripture quotations are from The ESV® Bible (The Holy Bible, English Standard Version®), copyright © 2001 by Crossway, a publishing ministry of Good News Publishers. Used by permission. All rights reserved.
Verses from the Quran: The Quran. Sahih International Translation, Al-Muntada al-Islami, 2004.
Any internet addresses (websites, blogs, etc.) are offered as a resource. They are not intended in any way to be or imply an endorsement by Gethsemane Press, nor does Gethsemane Press vouch for the content of these sites for the life of this book.

Cover Design: Author Photograph & art by Designer Sarah Earnest
Back Cover: Author Photograph --permission from Megan Larson Photography
Inside Cover page icon: common use
Chapter heading icon designed by author
Icons and pictures used within the book from creative common use
Other graphs and images used are cited.

Printed in the United States of America

*But when one turns to the Lord, the veil is removed. Now the*
*Lord is the Spirit, and where the Spirit of the Lord is, there is*
*freedom. And we all, with unveiled face, beholding the glory*
*of the Lord, are being transformed into the same image from*
*one degree of glory to another.*
*For this comes from the Lord who is the Spirit.*
*2 Corinthians 3:16-18 (ESV)*

May these words be pleasing to you, Lord. May they
glorify our Lord and Savior Christ Jesus and point only to
Him. Amen.

This book is dedicated to all the women who have influenced my life as a Muslim and even more in my new life as a Christian.

# Table of Contents

# Prologue - A Former Muslim's Perspective

As a Sunni Muslim woman, I was neither subjugated or oppressed. I never felt like I was forced to live below the standard of society by my family or community (and I lived the first part of my life in several Islamic countries). I realize now that I was pampered, sheltered and kept relatively uninformed about the deeper matters of faith. My parents were highly educated and only had daughters– no sons to take on the banner of Islam in the household or to carry on the family's name. My mother blazed new trails as a practicing physician. Both my father and mother raised us like boys in regard to having access to education, and we were given more freedoms than other women I knew. We could talk loudly (not rudely), be outgoing and we were unafraid of social constraints. We were pushed and encouraged to pursue an American University education and graduate degrees, which we obtained. We were raised with the freedom to have a western, independent mindset. From my background, it's easy to see that I did not have what the West would consider to be a traditional Muslim upbringing - not in the least.

Even though my parents tried their best to not have a dividing line between privileges set aside for men versus women, as I grew up, I became aware of society's standards in Muslim countries. My first memory of realizing there were different rules for boys and girls in Islam was in Saudi Arabia. Our family was invited to a huge wedding party at a venue. All of us entered the festive locale together and the women were shown by the attendants to a separate room, while the men made their way to another. Being little, I secretly hung on tight to my father's traditional white Saudi robes and quietly disappeared with him to the men's area. The men noticed the shy, four-year-old interloper immediately, but all had smiles, were kind and cordial. I don't think my father even realized that I had sneaked in behind him. The room was full of men of all ages. They were drinking hot tea from elaborately carved, long spouted brass and glass Arab teapots and of course, there was an enormous quantity of food laid out on engraved brass platters on low tables or on the carpets before them. The food kept coming as some of the men asked my father politely to get me out of there and back into the women's area. I was confused because in our home, there was no separation of sexes - even when we entertained in a large group. I was brought to the women's area and was dropped off at the door so that the maid in attendance could take me in. My mother laughed because she knew I had run off to be with my father.

There were no repercussions, just a quiet delineation of the fact that Muslim men and women do not gather together in social settings.

This separation was new to me and as the days passed, my awareness of the divide became more developed. When venturing outside the home, most women had a mahram (guardian - more on that in later chapters) and did not drive an automobile or travel on their own. Suddenly, life began to look a little bit different for this safely secluded little Muslim girl. I noticed for the first time that women were veiled outside the home. This might seem as a ridiculous observation to some, but children are kept indoors most of the time. The weather is blazing hot in the Middle East and the entertainment is usually kept within one another's homes. Our upstairs neighbors were Fatin and Busaina. They were two women who were kind, gentle, full of laugher, generous with their love and affection. Our families had relative freedom in going from one apartment to the other daily. I loved to visit them often because they had lots of snacks and they kept parrots!

I enjoy reminiscing and speaking about my life in the East, especially with my American audiences. There is something very exotic about a culture that tends to keep to itself. There is a built-in curiosity about the women who are veiled and "wear their religion on the outside" in their demeanor and dress. My experience growing into adulthood in the United States as a Muslim woman was different than what others have experienced. It is my desire to help the reader understand some common belief systems that exist in Islam, while trying to not make too many broad-brushed statements about every Muslim having the same set of values or assumptions.

Islam is not a monolithic religion. Those in the West have different views than the Easterners. Muslims born in the United States have different views than their immigrant parents. To add to the complexity, cultural influences have crept into how Muslims view Islam and how traditions are practiced. For example, I see things differently in the customs of marriage and family than my friends from Bangladesh or friends from Syria. However, there are general, underlying beliefs and principles many Muslims follow.

It is easy to get confused when discussing Islamic principles. Even Muslims can have ambiguity on whether a topic is from the Quran or from a tradition (Sunnah or Hadith) or are they cultural restraints being placed upon the Muslims who live in a particular country. These differences also extend to whether or not the Muslim person is a Sunni or a Shia. Even the Hadith are different for these two groups! These ambiguities can become intermingled with life, tradition, culture and religion. In my writing, I want to present what most Muslims in my own family and community believed. A common statement Muslims make is that the low value placed upon women could be due to the society and not due to Islam.

Our set of beliefs as a family are usually held by Southeastern Asian Muslims. Those from the Middle East or Africa may not know or understand where I am coming from due to their own traditions in culture. For this reason, it is important to define the background perspective used by the author. I was born in the Middle East and was raised there, along with years of schooling received in Pakistan. I moved to the United States as an immigrant when I was ten years old. My view of Islam is unique because I have both eastern and western eyes and I am blessed because I can walk the boundary line between these two cultures and religions. In 2007, I was saved by Jesus Christ, my Lord and Savior. I appreciate the ability God gave me to view Islam through my own Muslim experience of thirty-five years (well into adulthood) and to reflect upon it now with an understanding of who Jesus Christ is in my life. This is not something I take for granted and I know that the Lord has placed me in a unique position to share it with others. He created me for this purpose – to educate and equip others to learn about Islam from someone who has firsthand knowledge of it and has lived in several Muslim countries. May my perspectives and experience help the reader to understand and bridge differences between cultures and beliefs. The Bible reiterates this truth in my life in Ephesians 2:10 – "For we are his workmanship, created in Christ Jesus for good works, which God prepared beforehand, that we should walk in them (ESV)."

The main purpose of writing this book is to answer frequently asked questions about the hidden life of Muslim women. My American friends have many questions about the women who live behind the veil of Islam. The book is intended for Christians, however if any of my Muslim sisters are reading this, I welcome you to reach out to me personally so we can discuss these topics openly and honestly.

When the book was still in the conceptual phase, I was asked to write about women in the Quran. Since only Mary, mother of Jesus, is mentioned in the Quran it would have been a more thorough approach to research women in Islam as a whole. To this end, I wanted to compare and contrast Christianity and Islam through the main figures that represent each religion – Christ and Muhammad. Over the years, Muslims have argued with me that Muhammad does not represent Islam. That may be their stance, but it is the perception of many in the West that all of Islam hinges upon Muhammad. He is also mentioned in the shahada, the Muslim profession of faith or creed of Islam. Every Muslim testifies the Shahada in Arabic that "There is no God but Allah, and Muhammad is his messenger." For this reason, he is inseparable, especially in this discussion of women. The first part of this book will discuss Muhammad and Islam. Throughout the book, I tried to not misrepresent the Quran or the Hadith. there may be long passages presented so they are not taken out of context. There is nothing more irritating to me as a Christian when others take one line out of the Bible and try to use it out of context without supporting Scripture.

The later part of this book focuses on Jesus and His interactions with women. Since Jesus was never married, there are no wives to discuss. In the same chapter, I wanted to digress a little to discuss Eve, since she was addressed in the Islam section and I also think she is an interesting figure to many women, in Islam and Christianity.

## My Struggle

My first book "From Isa to Christ" was a testimony of my life that seemed to fly off the tips of my fingers and onto my computer screen. Authoring this book was an entirely different process. I knew when I was writing the first book that I would have to write another to fully explain all the nuances of being a woman in Islam. There were too many details I felt I needed to address, and all that information needed to be placed in a separate book dedicated to women.

I wanted to be thorough in my study and not misrepresent what a Muslim believes. This desire was born out of two reasons: the first is because I respect my family and their beliefs. The second reason is that I personally wanted to increase my breadth of knowledge in order to address the issues that exist for women across cultures and answer questions that come my way, especially from women in the West.

What happened as a result of this desire to learn and research was that I got terribly bogged down into a quagmire of Islamic literature. I spent a great amount of time reviewing the "Reliance of the Traveler" Sharia Law (a book about three inches thick) and then almost a year spent dissecting the Life of Muhammad (Sira) and then another year trying to write these findings in a comprehensive manner. Both books were so heavily detailed in their scope that it almost overwhelmed me. There is a great deal of information that the average Muslim doesn't know about... I used to be one of those Muslims.

Added to the details from the books was all the research that went into presenting the information to the best of my ability. That not only included finding research that supported my own views, but also information from Islamic websites that would help to support current Muslim views. This had another outcome I was not expecting and that was challenging my own views I was taught as a Muslim – again, not all Muslims believe the same thing, so some of the traditions I was taught were supported and at other times, I found no grounds for them either in the Quran or the Hadith. I even found several places where Imams and clerics who ran reliable Muslim websites couldn't answer what passages or verses meant. On top of all this, I tried to present information from real Muslim women and writings of Muslim women in order to show a variety of background and opinion in their views of Islam. Even with all this, I understand that some of what I have presented will not be palatable to Muslims or to Christians. I simply hope that I have tried to be as respectful as possible, while relaying facts that are difficult to process.

I found myself taking breaks from all the reading to reconfigure my mind and allow Christ's light to shine through His word, the Bible. I also began to memorize scripture again, starting with 1 Corinthians 13 -- the passage on love as defined by God and then by memorizing the entire book of Ephesians. This helped me to refocus on my task of writing and allowed my mind to go back to the place of peace that only comes from Christ Jesus, the Prince of Peace.

There is great darkness in the world. There is a new day that dawns when the light and life in the word of God shines through to others who do not know the beauty of Christ's sacrifice on the cross for us.

I hope this book will cause the Christian and Muslim reader to think about their religion, beliefs and allegiance to God Almighty. I also hope that this information and research will benefit the body of Christ in furthering the Great Commission (Matthew 28). May the work of my hands glorify you, O Lord.

# Chapter I

# Introduction to Islam

The beginnings of Islam are a baseline for understanding Islamic society today. It is sometimes difficult to separate out what is culture, tradition, history and religion. This introduction is not meant to be a comprehensive undertaking of an academic research treatise on the history of Islam but is intended to introduce the basics, especially the influence of Muhammad in the foundation of the religion.

## Background

The Arabian Peninsula has always been home to nomadic people called the Bedouins. There were many tribes that routinely battled one another for dominance and groups were constantly on the move. The pagan religion was predominant, with many who

worshipped idols (although in Persia, Zoroastrianism had existed
for centuries prior). There was some influence from both the
Arabian Jews (residing mostly in Yathrib - later named Medina)
and the Coptic Christians present in Egypt. This is the world into
which Muhammad (Arabic:محمد ; pronounced [muḣammad];
alternative English spelling is Mohammad), the founder and
prophet of Islam was born in 570 AD. He was the only son of
Abd Allah bin Al-Muttalib and Amina bint Wahb[1]. His name is
also Messenger of Allah ﷺ [the little symbol design at the end is
Arabic for "Peace Be Upon Him (PBUH)", which is a Muslim
designation of respect].

Abd Allah died before Muhammad's birth and Muhammad
was raised by his mother Amina, who in keeping with tradition,
gave her son at an early age to a wet nurse named Halima who
came from the nomadic tribe of the Sa'd ibn Bakr. His mother
died from illness just a few years later. Thus, he was orphaned by
the age of six and was given into the care of his paternal
grandfather, Abdul Al-Muttalib in Mecca. During that time,
Mecca was Arabia's most important pilgrimage hub for idol
worship and Abdul Al-Muttalib was a famous and most respected
leader. He controlled important pilgrimage concessions and
frequently presided over Mecca's Council of Elders. Tragically,
when Muhammad was eight his stately grandfather died and once
again, he was given into the care of another family member-- his

---

[1] http://www.religionfacts.com/muhammad

businessman uncle, Abu Talib. His paternal uncle put him to work on his camel caravan and they traveled together between Syria and Arabia on a merchant trade route. There, he gained wide exposure to various religious practices, storytelling, folklore and was especially interested in the teachings and traditions of the Jews and Christians[23]

**Muhammad's name in Arabic Calligraphy**

## Islamic Terminology

There are a few words that will be utilized throughout the book. The first is **Islam**, which means "to submit" in Arabic. The next commonly misused term to define is **Muslim**, which defines the person and means "one who submits" to the will of Allah as revealed in the Quran (the book). Islam is the religion and Muslim is the one who follows Islam, or the submitter. One cannot be a Muslim and not believe in the fundamental creed (called the Shahada) that states "There is no god but Allah, and Muhammad is his messenger." In order to be politically correct

---

[2] Lings, M. (1983) Muhammad: His Life Based on the Earliest Sources
[3] Figure: Muhammad name in Calligraphy by Abdelghani (2012) - Wikimedia Commons

and minimize the impact of Islam through the centuries, the
Western media has routinely misled the public by repeating that
"Islam means peace." It is factual that the word "Islam," by
technical definition does not mean peace and the root word in
Arabic comes only from the word submission. This message is
consistent with caliphs from the Middle East along with an
atheist named Sam Harris[4], who collectively assert that Islam is
not about peace, but that the goal is to bring about the submission
of all who do not believe in Islam, stated by Surah al Anfal (8:39)
"And fight them until there is no fitnah and [until] the religion,
all of it, is for Allah . And if they cease - then indeed, Allah is
Seeing of what they do."

The **Quran** (القرآن or alternative spelling - Koran) is the Holy
Book for Muslims. In Arabic, the word "Quran" means
"recitation." The Quran is divided into 114 chapters called **Surah**
in Arabic and verses called **Ayah**. In its entirety, the Quran is
shorter than the length of the New Testament.

Many people (including cultural Muslims) believe that the
Quran is the only book for guidance of a Muslim. This is what I
was taught and believed into adulthood as a Muslim. There is
much confusion in non-chronological presentation of chapters in
the Quran. For the reader, it is difficult to figure out what
occurred before and after verses of revelation to Muhammad

---

[4] Harris, S. (5 May 2008). "Losing Our Spines to Save Our
Necks". Huffingtonpost.com. Retrieved 19 March 2011. (updated 25 May
2011)

from Allah, especially when reading passages about battles in which the prophet was involved. Not only is the Quran missing contextual information in many areas, it is arranged from the longest to the shortest chapter (except for Surah Fatiha which is "the Opening or the Beginning"), which can confuse the reader by presenting later chronological passages, mixed in with earlier passages. There is further lack of clarity due to choppy wording and sentence structure.

For the Muslim, the Quran is given highest importance but there are two other sets of indispensable writings to consider when looking at Islam as a whole: the Quran, the Sira and the Hadith (in order of importance). The **Sira** (Sira سيرة means life or journey) is the account of the life of Muhammad - the ultimate prophet of Allah. It gives context to the historical aspects of Islam and easily, Muslim clerics believe that the most trustworthy writer of the Sira was a historian by the name of Ibn Ishaq (704 AD to 768 AD), whose work was then translated by Alfred Guillaume. It mainly chronicles the ancestry, childhood, marriages, and the battles of Muhammad and has details about Muhammad's military career and conquests that led to the growth of Islam. It is important to note that there is much uncertainty about any records prior to these, therefore it is believed to be the earliest biographical source. According to Guillaume, the original text of the Sīrat Rasūl Allāh by Ibn Ishaq did not survive. What we have today is some of the original text that was copied over into a work by Ibn Hisham.[5] Muslims tend to avoid any translations, especially one done by a Westerner (Alfred Guillaume was a British scholar with an impressive list of Ivy League credentials) due to bias, yet the Muslims I know have never read or even heard of the Sira.

The third set of important writings is called the Hadith. The word **Hadith** (حديث) in Arabic means "report" or "narrative." Hadith is important because these statements were written down by followers after Muhammad would have his Quranic revelation from Allah. Whatever he spoke during these revelation episodes was a part of the Quran, but what he spoke after (usually to explain the revelation) was written into the Hadith. The sheer volume of the Hadith is overwhelming with over 6,800 traditions[6] that may repeat.

Together, the Quran, Sira and the Hadith make up a trilogy of reference that can help one make a more scholarly examination of Islam. Without each piece, there is only a part of information presented that can be confusing, misinterpreted and downright misleading. The Hadith writings are also important because along with the Quran, they make up the **Sharia** laws for Muslim nations. Sharia means "path to water" in Arabic, indicating that these are the rules man needs in order to sustain life. The word

---

[5] The Life of Muhammad, a translation of Ishaq's Sirat Rasul Allah, with introduction and notes by A. Guillaume (1955). Oxford University Press, Great Clarendon Street, Oxford.
[6] https://www.politicalislam.com/trilogy-project/

for law in Arabic is fiqh which would be closer to the idea of an established legal system of interpreting and applying Sharia.

Author and researcher Dr. Bill Warner (founder of the Center for Study of Political Islam) provides fascinating research into each book with a study of the words, verses and information in each Islamic text. On his website, he breaks down the sizes of each book and provides a visual diagram (see figure):[7]:

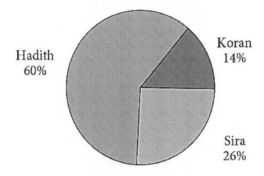

**Bill Warner – Relative Size of Islam's Trilogy Texts**

## Abrogation

To add to the confusion of the multiple writings is the notion of "abrogation," which means to repeal or an annulment of an earlier verse. Abrogation occurs several times in the Quran, usually when the earlier, more peaceful passages in the Quran were later replaced by stricter and more forceful verses. Cultural Muslims who have not read the Quran can get agitated when presented with this information and tend to blame others for this variation

---

[7] Warner, B. "The Islamic Doctrine of Women." CSPI
http://cspipublishing.com/statistical/TrilogyStats/The_Relative_Sizes_of_the_
Trilogy_Texts.html

in text. Abrogation is not a concept, or a claim made up by unbelievers but is something that the Quran itself attests to in Surah Al Nahl 16:101:

> "And when We substitute a verse in place of a verse - and Allah is most knowing of what He sends down - they say, "You, [O Muhammad], are but an inventor [of lies]." But most of them do not know."[8]

It seems like Muhammad himself was being put to task by those around him when there were inconsistencies in the revelations he reported to others.

Here is one example of abrogation, where a peaceful passage was replaced with a more violent verse. In Surah 53:29 a command is given for how Muslims should treat those who do not believe in Islam- "Therefore shun those who turn away from Our Message and desire nothing but the life of this world." This passage was later abrogated by the infamous "verse of the sword" in Surah 9:5 that states:

> "And when the sacred months have passed, then kill the polytheists wherever you find them and capture them and besiege them and sit in wait for them at every place of ambush. But if they should repent, establish prayer, and give zakat, let them [go] on their way. Indeed, Allah is Forgiving and Merciful."[9]

This is where the lack of chronological order to the Quran makes it difficult to know what passage came first and when the abrogation came. Perhaps this is why Muslim scholars believe it

---

[8] Quran Surah Al Nahl - https://quran.com/16/101
[9] Quran Surah At Tawbah - https://quran.com/9/5-15

is best to let the professionals do the work of interpreting the Quran.

## Use of Brackets in the Quran Translation

There are brackets included in the English translation of the Quran and according to Muslim clerics[10]

> "Sometimes, there are meanings in the Arabic language that contain nuances which cannot be expressed in English. Sometimes, the context from the previous verses or verses following it reveals a meaning not discernable by just looking at the verse itself. In such occasions, brackets have been carefully used."

This book will attempt to present complete verses when possible, including brackets used by accepted sources of English translation of the Quran, including: Sahih International, Mohammed Pickthall, and Yusuf Ali. Most of the verses used are from the Quran - Sahih International Translation (2004), so they are not referenced separately (but are cited in the copyright and publication page at the beginning of this book). As a Christian who reads extensively, I do not appreciate verses taken out of context from the Bible and therefore do not wish to take out verses from the Quran or the Hadith out of context either, especially regarding information to which a Muslim might take objection.

---

[10] https://www.quranicpath.com/quranicpath/FAQ.html

**Language of Heaven?**

Ignorance was bliss for me as a Muslim because I had not read the Quran until I was in my thirties. Muslims typically spend time reciting the Quran, but many do not read to understand the meaning of the passages. If they have read the Quran, most likely they've read it in Arabic. If they've read it in Arabic, it is important to know that over 84% of the Muslim world doesn't speak Arabic as their mother tongue (only Muslims in the Middle East and parts of northern Africa speak Arabic).

In Surah Yusuf 12:2, it states "Indeed, We have sent it down as an Arabic Qur'an that you might understand," Surah Maryam 19:97 "So, [O Muhammad], We have only made Qur'an easy in the Arabic language that you may give good tidings thereby to the righteous and warn thereby a hostile people," and in Surah Fussilat 41:3 "A Book whose verses have been detailed, an Arabic Qur'an for a people who know…" along with several other verses that state Arabic is the main language of the Quran.

In order to fulfill a works requirements, they have been asked to "read" and recite the Quran in Arabic by their local mosque leader. By the way, that is the only way a Muslim is allowed to read it, for Arabic is considered to be the language of Heaven. The claim is that if one reads the Quran in a translated language, it will not give the exact meaning because it is not in Arabic. Even the most scholarly person would not know what the Quran says unless read in the manner it was given to Muhammad - in Arabic. The Muslims who don't speak Arabic **do not** actually understand what are the meaning of the phrases they recite in their daily prayers or in the reading of the Quran. This means that Pakistanis, Malaysians and even Americans who do not know Arabic still have to pray, read, and listen to the verses of the Quran in the ancient Arabic.

Chances are that in any mosque across the United States on any given Friday (Jum'ah) afternoon, prayers and sermons (khutbah) are being conducted in Arabic, without most of the attendees understanding what is being said. According to Harvard Divinity School:

> "While it is possible to translate the Arabic text of the Quran into other languages, Muslims generally consider translations to be interpretations and not the Quran itself. It is important to note that no one translation can claim to present the Quran exactly as found in Arabic; translations can change meanings, gloss over complexities that are found in the original, and are unable to transmit the aesthetic dimensions of the text.[11]"

Even in conversations with Muslim women who speak Arabic as their native tongue, the antiquated language with odd accent marks and punctuation presents linguistic issues. A comparison could be made with Christians using the King James Version (KJV) instead of a more contemporary English version, although the KJV was written in 1611, while the oldest existing copy of the Quran is from the 9th century (making the Quran's language even older!). Anachronistic language has its own issues and

---

[11] Harvard Divinity School. Religious Literacy Project. Qur'an: The word of God. Retrieved online https://rlp.hds.harvard.edu/religions/islam/quran-word-god

complexities, with archaic words and phrases that make
translation difficult and cumbersome – even for a native speaker.
Even with native Arabic speakers, it is not uncommon to find that
they have not read the Quran.

**Islam is not Monolithic**

While Islam attests to faith in Allah and all belong to one
community called the "ummah," there is great diversity within
the religion. There is an incorrect assumption made by the
mainstream media that all Muslims hold the same ideology.
There are different understandings due to culture and
geographical beliefs. There are two main divisions in Islam that
arose after Muhammad's death in 632 AD: **Sunni and Shia**.
There are much smaller sects that came later such as the Sufi and
Ahmadiyya that are usually dismissed by orthodox Muslims as
not being representative of Islamic beliefs. The Sunni Muslims
are those who believe in a caliphate (first caliph -Abu Bakr) after
Muhammad's death. Their name comes from the word Sunnah
(Arabic سنة), which means "habits or customs" -- different from
Sunni (sect). They also include the Hanafi and Hanbali
(Wahaabi) schools of jurisprudence that defines the stricter
orthodoxy of Islam. They were also the first group to codify the
Sharia laws around the tenth century.

Shia (Arabic شِيعَة ) Muslims are those who believed that Ali,
Muhammad's first cousin and closest living male relative (as well
as his son-in-law, having married his daughter Fatima), should

have inherited Muhammad's rule due to his double relationship with Muhammad. The word Shia means "group or party of" Ali in Arabic.

He was considered to be the first Imam of Islam by the Shia and they claim that Ali was featured in several Hadiths for his service to Muhammad in many ways. He was assassinated in 661 AD. It might be interesting to point out that both sects use a separate set of Hadith. This also accounts for the variations in law and Islamic rulings in Shia countries like Iraq and Iran. Since I used to be a Sunni Muslim and they represent close to 90% of the Muslim world (including Saudi Arabia), I will mainly use the Sunni Hadith[12] for a reference in this book.

---

[12] http://www.pewforum.org/2009/10/07/mapping-the-global-muslim-population/

# Chapter 2

# Women in Islam - History

In my discussions with Westerners about Islam and Muhammad, there is a piqued interest about women. The general consensus is that women hold a different place in Islam and there is not much else known about them. There was not open discussion about women's issues in the various Muslim communities where we lived. I had been a part of some hushed conversations as a Muslim about Muhammad's wives. Some Muslim women choose to talk about them openly, even reveling in the fact that he chose them to be in his household, while other Muslim women have disdain for not just Muhammad's wives but for the inevitable discussion of polygamy in Islam that follows. Islamic clerics' view is that the wives of Muhammad should be given a place of honor and special consideration when studying Islam. With the advent of the internet, much of this information is now available

at your fingertips. Again, the information presented in this
chapter is provided from the Sira, Hadith and any Quranic Surahs
associated with them.

## Women in Muhammad's Life

There were many women who influenced Muhammad during
his life. There is not much known about his mother, Amina, but
the Sira of Muhammad supplies clues about the influence his wet
nurse, Halima, had on him. One record is from his childhood
where the young boy Muhammad told Halima about an incident
where he saw a vision where two men dressed in white opened up
his chest and took out his heart (he saw that it had a black
marking on it). In dismay, the wet nurse looked where the boy
was pointing on his body and confirmed there was a large mark
on his back, found between his shoulder blades (according to
Hadith, it was raised skin the size of a pigeon's egg with moles
and hairs on it. Muslims call it the "seal of prophethood").[13]
Shaking and afraid of what this might mean, she told his mother
Amina about the incident. His own mother asked "Tell me truly
what is with you, tell me the truth! I will not let you go until you
have told me what has happened. Is it that you fear the Devil for
him?" "Yes" said Halima.[14] Further corroborating Halima's story
was Anas Ibn Malik, the prophet's companion, who provided an

---

[13] https://islamqa.info/en/answers/22725/description-of-the-seal-of-
prophethood
[14] Lings, M. (1983) Muhammad: His Life Based on the Earliest Sources. Sira

account in Sahih Muslim Hadith (1/167 Book 162). Here, he said
that the cutting up of his heart did indeed leave a physical scar in
the shape of a line on Muhammad's chest.

> "Anas b. Malik reported that Gabriel came to the Messenger of
> Allah (ﷺ) while he was playing with his playmates. He took
> hold of him and lay him prostrate on the ground and tore open
> his breast and took out the heart from it and then extracted a
> blood-clot out of it and said:
> That was the part of Satan in thee. And then he washed it with the
> water of Zamzam in a golden basin and then it was joined together
> and restored to its place. The boys came running to his mother,
> i.e. his nurse and said: Verily Muhammad has been murdered.
> They all rushed toward him (and found him all right) His color
> was changed, Anas said. I myself saw the marks of needle on
> his breast."[15]

The nurse was so fearful that the Devil had cut him, that she did
not want to care for him any further and returned the child back
to his mother.

After his mother's untimely death, he was again given into
the care of his grandfather so he could have a greater male
influence from his adolescence into adulthood. He then went
under the tutelage of his prosperous uncle Abu Talib who
subsequently introduced him to the bustling merchant trade,
business, accounting and how to turn a profit for the family. It is
reported in numerous Islamic writings that Muhammad was
known for being trustworthy and was influential in his dealings
with others.

---

[15] Sahih Muslim Hadith 162, 320 Retrieved https://sunnah.com/muslim/1/320

### Khadija bint Khawalayd

It was exactly this reputation in business that caught the eye of Khadija bint Khawalayd. At twenty-five years of age, he married the noble (she was from the aristocratic tribe of Quraysh) and wealthy widow Khadija from Mecca after handling business transactions for her. She was forty years old and a great supporter of Muhammad - both in finances and in religion. It is said that she was his first convert to Islam.

Muslims regard Khadija as the "mother of all believers." She is given honor and esteem, not just by Muslims but also by Muhammad's own testimony about her. Muslims also are proud of her career as a businesswoman who owned property with which she helped Muhammad launch his career.

Here are several Hadith traditions about Khadija:

*Volume 5, Book 58, Number 164:*

Narrated 'Aisha:
> "I did not feel jealous of any of the wives of the Prophet as much as I did of Khadija (although) she died before he married me, for I often heard him mentioning her, and Allah had told him to give her the good tidings that she would have a palace of Qasab (i.e. pipes of precious stones and pearls in Paradise), and whenever he slaughtered a sheep, he would send her women-friends a good share of it."

*Volume 5, Book 58, Number 165:*

Narrated 'Aisha:
> "I did not feel jealous of any woman as much as I did of Khadija because Allah's Apostle used to mention her very often. He married me after three years of her death, and his Lord (or Gabriel) ordered him to give her the good news of having a palace of Qasab in Paradise."

*Volume 5, Book 58, Number 166:*

Narrated 'Aisha:
> "I did not feel jealous of any of the wives of the Prophet as much as I did of Khadija though I did not see her, but the Prophet used to mention her very often, and whenever he slaughtered a sheep, he would cut its parts and send them to the women friends of Khadija. When I sometimes said to him, "(You treat Khadija in such a way) as if there is no woman on earth except Khadija," he would say, "Khadija was such-and-such, and from her I had children."

*Volume 5, Book 58, Number 167:*

Narrated Ismail:
> "I asked 'Abdullah bin Abi Aufa, "Did the Prophet give glad tidings to Khadija?" He said, "Yes, of a palace of Qasab (in Paradise) where there will be neither any noise nor any fatigue."

Muhammad had a quiet and monogamous marriage with Khadija until she died twenty-five years later. They had several children, both boys and girls. All children, except for their youngest daughter Fatima, died in childhood. She also had a young house slave named Zayd (also spelled Zaid), whom she gave as a gift to her husband in marriage. Muhammad soon adopted him and claimed him publicly as his own son.

According to noted author Abdul-Haqq,[16] there were Christians in Muhammad's extended family - Warqa (also spelled Waraqa or Warqah) bin Naufal and Uthman bin al-Huwayrith were cousins of Khadija. Around the age of forty, tradition has it that Muhammad was secluded in a cave, as was his habit to go

---

[16] Abdul Haqq, Abdiyah Akbar (1980). Sharing your faith with a Muslim. Bethany Fellowship, Inc.

for a time of reflection, called Hira. He was then visited by the angel Gabriel (Arabic: Jibril) who began the process of revealing the Quran to him.[17]

He was quite agitated and nervous when he came back and began to worry that spirits of the air had possessed him. He was troubled to the point of suicide and his own story is noted in Al-Tabari's[18] book: "I shall go to some high mountain cliff and cast myself down there from so that I may kill myself and be at rest. I went off with this in mind, but when I was in the midst of the mountains, I heard a voice from heaven saying, "O Muhammad, thou art God's apostle and I am Gabriel."

After this revelation, he still sought his wife Khadija to determine if he was a prophet or was one demon-possessed, for he was not certain. She brought her cousin Warqa who said that maybe he had a revelation by Gabriel who had come to Moses and had a mission to his own people as a prophet. While Khadija became a convert, Warqa remained a Christian all his life. In the first year, Muhammad only had a handful of followers but in the following years, as the momentum grew so did the violence.

After Khadija's death, Muhammad went on to take ten more wives simultaneously. He also had at least two favorite female slaves. The Quran talks about his wives with honor, favor and praise. Surah Al Ahzab 33:6 relates:

---

[17]https://www.sahih-bukhari.com/Pages/Bukhari_9_87.php
[18] Al Tabari: Tarikh al-Rasul Wa al-Muluk. Leiden (1881).

"The Prophet is more worthy of the believers than themselves, and his wives are [in the position of] their mothers. And those of [blood] relationship are more entitled [to inheritance] in the decree of Allah than the [other] believers and the emigrants, except that you may do to your close associates a kindness [through bequest]. That was in the Book inscribed."

Despite having a whole harem of women at his convenience, only two of his women bore him children (Khadija, his first wife and his Christian slave Mary) and only one female child (Fatima) lived into adulthood. *No sons survived.*

Below is an account of each of Muhammad's women, including supporting verses from Islamic literature (mostly Hadith). They vary in background and age. This is an area which can be commonly misconstrued, as some Muslims do not have complete knowledge of how many wives Muhammad had (for the Quran allows four). A Hadith states:

*Sahih Bukhari Volume 1, Book 5, Number 268*

"Narrated Qatada: Anas bin Malik said, "The Prophet used to visit all his wives in a round, during the day and night and they were eleven in number." I asked Anas, "Had the Prophet the strength for it?" Anas replied, "We used to say that the Prophet was given the strength of thirty (men)." And Sa'id said on the authority of Qatada that Anas had told him about nine wives only (not eleven).[19]"

Given the consternation over the number of wives, there is not a lot of documentation presented in common Muslim literature about his concubines. The historian Al Tabari estimated that there

---

[19] Sahih al-Bukhari Vol. 1, Book of Bathing (Ghusl), Hadith 268 Retrieved online https://muflihun.com/bukhari/5/268

may have been up to fifteen women associated with Muhammad – eleven wives and four concubines. Traditionally in Arabia, the concubines were never given wife status, for sometimes they were acquired as slaves. They usually remained had undetermined privileges for they were below the status of a wife, but sometimes above the status of a slave.

## Muhammad's Women after Khadija
### *Sawda bint Zam'a*
Sawda was married previously and had suffered hardships due to becoming a Muslim. She was fifty-five years old and Muhammad was around fifty at the time. Many speculate that he married Sawda at the same time he was betrothed to Aisha, his child bride. There is a Hadith that he wanted to divorce her until she gave up her nights with him to his bride, Aisha.

### *Aisha bint Abu Bakr*
Aisha was the daughter of Muhammad's close friend and ally Abu Bakr. Muhammad alleged that he saw her as an infant in a dream.

Sahih Bukhari Hadith Volume 9 Book 87 No 139 & 140. Narrated 'Aisha:

> "Allah's Apostle said to me, "You were shown to me twice (in my dream) before I married you. I saw an angel carrying you in a silken piece of cloth, and I said to him, 'Uncover (her),' and behold, it was you. I said (to myself), 'If this is from Allah, then it must happen..."

*Sahih Bukhari Volume 5, Book 58, Number 236 (same as Sahih Bukhari Volume 7, Book 62, Number 88*

"Narrated Hisham's father: Khadija died three years before the Prophet departed to Medina. He stayed there for two years or so and then he married 'Aisha when she was a girl of six years of age, and he consummated that marriage when she was nine years old."

*Sahih Bukhari Volume 5, Book 58, Number 234*

"Narrated 'Aisha: The Prophet engaged me when I was a girl of six (years). We went to Medina and stayed at the home of Bani-al-Harith bin Khazraj. Then I got ill, and my hair fell down. Later on my hair grew (again) and my mother, Um Ruman, came to me while I was playing in a swing with some of my girlfriends. She called me, and I went to her, not knowing what she wanted to do to me. She caught me by the hand and made me stand at the door of the house. I was breathless then, and when my breathing became all right, she took some water and rubbed my face and head with it. Then she took me into the house. There in the house I saw some Ansari women who said, "Best wishes and Allah's Blessing and a good luck." Then she entrusted me to them, and they prepared me (for the marriage). Unexpectedly Allah's Apostle came to me in the forenoon and my mother handed me over to him, and at that time I was a girl of nine years of age."

The Hadith passage in 234 is from Aisha herself. She was an eye-witness to Muhammad and his preferences from what he liked to eat to the times he would meet with each of his wives. According to Ibn Hisham's biography, she was betrothed to Muhammad in Medina when she was six years old and the marriage was consummated when she was nine years old. Muhammad was fifty-three years old at the time.

It should be noted that historically, it was customary practice to have a betrothal as a promise to fulfill the marriage at a later time with physical relations. The usual tradition even today in some countries is that a betrothal holds the same status as a legal marriage without the physical consummation, which usually took place after the woman began puberty. Several Hadiths (as noted above) relate that she was allowed to bring her dolls to play with to the honeymoon and marriage bed-- even though Muhammad did not like images of man portrayed in any kind of a statue or form (he considered it to be a version of idolatry and had an abhorrence to manmade images).

*Sahih Bukhari Volume 8, Book 73, Number 151*

> "Narrated 'Aisha: I used to play with the dolls in the presence of the Prophet, and my girlfriends also used to play with me. When Allah's Apostle used to enter (my dwelling place) they used to hide themselves, but the Prophet would call them to join and play with me. (The playing with the dolls and similar images is forbidden, but it was allowed for 'Aisha at that time, as she was a little girl, not yet reached the age of puberty.) (Fateh-al-Bari page 143, Vol.13)"

Westerners ask me about the reasons why Muhammad would have married a little girl - they are shocked to learn that he didn't leave Aisha alone as a child of six and there is evidence in the Hadiths that he engaged in physical play with her. There are some very explicit sexual descriptions narrated candidly by Aisha that make it difficult to read as a woman and as one raised in the West (where a man's sexual relationship with a child is expressly forbidden, not to mention illegal). After reading these, I realized that this might have been the reason many women are not encouraged and sometimes downright forbidden to read the Hadith.

There are passages that are quite disturbing written by Islamic scholars who declare religious law or ruling called **"fatwa(h)s."** Fatwas are issued where there might be some confusion or debate on what the Quran states, so the Islamic scholars and leaders get together to decide on a ruling that goes out publicly to the Muslim world to give all Muslims guidance on how to follow the prophet's example. There are two fatwa numbered 31409 and 41409 (published 7/5/1421 Hijri) that contain the sexual information about the nature of Muhammad's physical relationship with Aisha. Due to the explicit and graphic nature of the descriptions, if you are interested in learning more, you can research the Arabic term *"mufa'khathat"* or the English term "thighing."

The larger problem at hand, however is the age of Aisha at the time – that doesn't even come into the explanation and is not expressly forbidden to Muslim men. The Quran does not give a minimum age for marriage, but only states in Surah 65:4:

"And those who no longer expect menstruation among your women - if you doubt, then their period is three months, and [also for] those who have not menstruated. And for those who are pregnant, their term is until they give birth. And whoever fears Allah - He will make for him of his matter ease."

Which means that men needed to wait until menstruation to consummate marriage – which is exactly what Muhammad did as an example for others to follow.

Since this is not a favorable view to take in the West (using children to satisfy sexual needs), Muslims are quick to defend these fatwas and state that they have been corrupted by evil infidels. Another objection raised is that the fatwas are old and do not apply today. According to a 2019 citation from the Islamic Fatwas[20] website, there is still no minimum age for marriage.

---

**The Suitable Age for Marriage**

QUESTION: What is the suitable age for marriage for men and women, because some young women do not accept marriage from those who are older than them? Likewise, some men do not marry women who are older than them...

ANSWER: I advise young women not to refuse marriage from a man due to his age, such as being ten, twenty or thirty years older than her. This is not a reason, because the Prophet, sallallaahu alayhi was salam, married 'A'ishah, may Allah be pleased with her, when he was fifty-three years old and she was a girl of nine years old. So being older does not harm. There is no sin in the woman being older, nor any sin in the man being older, because the Prophet, sallallaahu alayhi was salam, married Khadijah, may Allah be pleased with her, when she was forty years old and he was twenty-five years old, before the Revelation came to him, sallallaahu alayhi was salam; that is, she, may Allah be pleased with her, was fifteen years older than him. Then he married 'A'ishah, may Allah be pleased with her, when she was small -6 or 7 years old and he was 53 years old.

---

[20] http://www.fatwaislam.com/fis/index.cfm?scn=fd&ID=42

Many of those who speak on the radio or television deter people from marriage between men and women of differing ages - this is all wrong & saying such things is not permissible for them. It is obligatory for a woman to look at the (prospective) husband, and if he is righteous and suitable, she should agree, even if he is older than her... In short, the age should not be an excuse and it should not be considered something shameful, as long as the man is righteous, and the woman is righteous. May Allah reform the situation of us all. - Shaykh Abdul Azeez Bin Baz

Fatawa Islamiyah, volume 5, The Book of Marriage, page 169-170 (2019) FatwaIslam.com   Fatwa - Islamic Rulings - Islamic Scholars

As a defense to Islam, there are some Muslims who contend that non-canonical writings report that it was an elderly Isaac who married Rebekah when she was three years old (the Christian Bible does not say that -- in fact, the Bible states that she was a woman who was watering her father's camels when Abraham's servant approached her and spoke to her at the well about her family – Genesis 24). In addition, these unorthodox writings state that Mary, mother of Jesus was 12 while Joseph the carpenter was 90 years (obtained from the Roman Catholic Apocrypha – not a part of the Protestant Biblical Cannon and both rejected and refuted by Biblical scholars). Even if Muslims make the claim that there were child marriages in the Old Testament, the passages are not prescriptive for the way all Christians are to behave. That is the critical difference: Jesus

never married, nor took a child bride, nor prescribed it for His
followers to do so.

## A Note on Women's Sexuality

Topics of a sexual nature are rarely discussed with Muslim
women. Some Muslims go as far as to not discuss anything about
a woman's body, especially their insides (for some it means no
pictures of pregnancy ultrasounds, not even a doctor looking
down a woman's throat for sickness). They are protected in the
families as delicate hot-house flowers kept innocent until their
marriage day --which is not a terrible thing! After my marriage,
when I was expecting our first child, I was not allowed to say the
word "pregnancy" or mention things that were related to
childbirth around male members of the family or any other
Muslim men who might overhear. It is a matter of propriety,
manners, honor/shame and disrespect caused by bringing
attention to a woman's body or sexuality. I think sometimes
people forget that even in the United States, there are cultures
that do not openly discuss topics like this and consider them to be
taboo.

As I was growing up, I had absolutely *no knowledge* that
there was such explicit sexual detail written about Muhammad's
life until I became a Christian and today, with the internet
allowing one to freely research details, many can find out about
Islamic writings from all over the world. Muslims may argue
against these findings, saying that the Imams or clerics are the

ones who have knowledge and they are not written in the Quran, so it excludes them from the normal Muslim beliefs. The truth of the matter is that the writings do exist and moreover, are used for Islamic jurisprudence. Child marriage in Muslim countries exists as well and whether someone wants to debate if it is the "norm" is arbitrary to the fact. The "apostle of Allah" as the Quran text calls him, was said to have done this himself and he is still held up around the world as the one to emulate for all Muslim men. The Quran states in Surah al Ahzab 33:21 (emphasis mine): ***There has certainly been for you in the Messenger of Allah an excellent pattern for anyone*** whose hope is in Allah and the Last Day and [who] remembers Allah often."

Apart from these difficult passages, Aisha is heralded as an outspoken woman who freely shared her views on sexuality, marriage, Islamic traditions and she has narrated over two thousand Hadiths according to Islamiyat, a core text for Muslim Students. One can see her strong will, strength and her sense of humor as she dictated these passages. She is quite entertaining to read, and I found her detailed view of the early Muslim world to be intriguing and brutally honest. Even though she never bore any children, she went on to educate and serve the Muslim community in Arabia for forty-four years after Muhammad's death in 632 AD.[21]

---

[21]Aleem, S. (2007). "Prophet Muhammad(s) and His Family: A Sociological Perspective. AuthorHouse.

As one most intimate to Muhammad and having unlimited access to the proliferation of narrations about his traditions, it is remarkable what Aisha contributed to the body of knowledge of early Islam and an eyewitness to the establishment of Muslim practices. She truly shines as the most interesting and comprehensive when it came to reading Hadith. Her commentaries present an unabashed version of Islamic history and she seemed to be remarkably candid in her graphic descriptions of what occurred during Muhammad's time as an eyewitness. Even centuries later, her young, honest voice cannot be ignored.

### Hafsa bint Umar

She was the daughter of Muhammad's friend Umar ibn al-Khattab (he was also known as the second caliph)[22] and wife of Muslim companion Khunais ibn Hudhaifah. The details of her life are not well-known, other than she was widowed when her husband died at the Battle of Badr. Tradition has it that she was distraught and out of benevolence from the prophet who did not want to see her remain a widow, she was then married to Muhammad. Tradition holds that she helped to narrate sixty Hadiths.

---

[22] " Hafsa bint Umar." In The Oxford Dictionary of Islam. Ed. John L. Esposito. Oxford Islamic Studies Online. 26-Nov-2019. <http://www.oxfordislamicstudies.com/article/opr/t125/e763>.

### Zaynab bint Khuzayma

She was also widowed when her husband Ubayda ibn al-Harith, another companion and Muslim died at the Battle of Badr. She was called "mother to the poor" due to her charity work. The Battle of Badr was one of the pivotal battles fought at the inception of Islam against the pagans of Arabia. Muhammad also fought in the battle. She was one of the first wives to come from out of the esteemed family of Quraysh (along with Khadija).

### Hind bint Abi Umayya (Umm Salama)

She was a faithful Muslim woman who was also widowed when her husband died. She brought young children into the marriage. She was given status among the Muslim community as a teacher of the early Islamic laws.

### Zaynab bint Jahsh

Zaynab was the wife of Muhammad's adopted son Zayd ibn Harithah (Khadijah's slave that she gifted to Muhammad and he later adopted). She was also Muhammad's biological cousin (her mother was sister to Muhammad's father). Tradition holds that Muhammad visited their home unexpectedly one day and saw her dressed in a thin gossamer gown which revealed her body as she rushed to greet him when he arrived at their door. That was the moment he became infatuated with Zaynab's delicate white skin and beauty, thus Zayd was pressured into a divorce through a revelation in the Quran.

Muslims hotly protest this view of the relationship. Their main argument is that it was Muhammad himself who arranged the marriage for his adopted son. If he wanted her himself, he would have married her to begin with and not given her a dowry that he paid for his son. That argument would stand if there weren't a few verses in the Quran that show this was a fragile situation. At Muhammad's time, the pagans in Arabia considered adopted sons to be legal, legitimate sons in all rights and manner. To marry his son's wife would be incest. Therefore, the timing of this action was curious. Upon the request from his father, Zayd at once acquiesced to a divorce (the marriage lasted less than two years total). Shortly after the divorce, to justify marrying her, Muhammad announced the new revelations that since his adopted son did not count as a real biological son, so followed that his now ex-wife Zaynab was not really his daughter-in-law, and conveniently as a prophet, he was allowed more than the standard four wives as dictated in the Quran in Surah 4:3 that states:

> "And if you fear that you will not deal justly with the orphan girls, then marry those that please you of [other] women, two or three or four. But if you fear that you will not be just, then [marry only] one or those your right hand possesses. That is more suitable that you may not incline [to injustice]."

Another revelation addressed Zayd's position as a legitimate son:

> "Nor has He (Allah) made your adopted sons your sons. Such is (only) your (manner of) speech by your mouths. But God tells the truth, and He shows the way. Call them by (the names of) their fathers, that is better in the sight of God" (Surah 33:5).

To further solidify the claim, one more revelation from the Quran gave a green light to the marriage of Zaynab to Muhammad in Surah Al Ahzab 33:37:

> "And [remember, O Muhammad], when you said to the one on whom Allah bestowed favor and you bestowed favor, "Keep your wife and fear Allah," while you concealed within yourself that which Allah is to disclose. And you feared the people, while Allah has more right that you fear Him. So, when Zayd had no longer any need for her, We married her to you in order that there not be upon the believers any discomfort concerning the wives of their adopted sons when they no longer have need of them. And ever is the command of Allah accomplished."[23]

It is distressing to note that these passages posed a notable change in the status of orphans and fatherless children in Islam. After the revelation, Zayd changed his name back to his original name as Zayd ibn Harithah and gave up the adopted name he had since childhood of Zayd ibn Muhammad.

The new revelations from Allah set one more standard for all of Islam to follow that adopted children will never attain the true status in a family as biological children. They do not have the same rights and the rights they are given can be rejected or repealed at any time. The concept of "Mahrameyat" in Islam is that you can live and be near the opposite gender only if they are related through blood and marriage. This creates another adoption issue for Muslims with children who have gone through puberty. An adopted male would need to be chaperoned when

---

[23] Quran Surah Al Ahzab https://quran.com/33/36-46

around females of the household because there is no blood relation and therefore, he (or the females) cannot be trusted. Also, an adopted child also is not allowed to inherit from the parents, as they are not their bona fide child. Again, this was not the existing standard in the Arab world prior to Muhammad's revelation and marked a change in societal laws that exist today.

### *Juwayriyya bint al-Harith*

Juwayriyya was taken as a captive from one of the many military skirmishes. She was the twenty-year-old daughter of an Arab Chief and the family insisted that she should be released as a prisoner. Muhammad 'Ali Qutb's book, "Women Around the Messenger" states:

> "The mother of the faithful 'A'ishah (may Allah be pleased with her) speaks about that day: The Messenger of Allah (peace be upon him) took the women of Banu al-Mustaliq as captives. He took out the one fifth of them and divided the remaining ones among his Companions giving the cavalry soldier two shares and the infantry soldier a share. Juwayriyah (may Allah be pleased with her) fell into the share of Thabit ibn Qays al-Ansari. She was formerly married to a cousin of hers known as Mani' ibn Safwan ibn Malik ibn Judhaymah, who is also known as Dhu ash- Shafrah. She was bereaved of him. She then agreed with Thabit ibn Qays [who was one of Muhammad's companions] to buy her freedom with nine Ooqiyah."[24]

To put it simply, she and her father tried to purchase her freedom from one of Muhammad's friends, but Muhammad (fifty-eight years old at the time) said that instead of taking the ransom and

---

[24] Qutb, Muhammad 'Ali. "Women Around the Messenger" Translated by 'Abdur Rafi' Adewale Imam. (n.d.). International Islamic Publishing House.

then turning around to pay a dowry, that he, himself would marry her instead, since his eye had fallen upon her in favor.

> "'A'ishah describes her saying, "She was a pleasant woman. No one saw her except he became captivated by her. While the Messenger of Allah (peace be upon him) was there when suddenly Juwayriyah entered asking him concerning her ransom agreement (with Thabit). By Allah, as soon as I saw her, I disliked her entering the place of Messenger of Allah (peace be upon him) for I knew that he would see what I saw in her."

As a wedding gift, Muhammad released one hundred of her clan members from slavery.[25]

### *Safiyya bint Huyeiy Ibn Akhtab*

During the time of Muhammad's reign in Arabia, there were many Jews who led great families and their businesses prospered. Safiyya was the daughter of the chief of the large Jewish tribe Banu Nadir. As documented in Islamic sources, her husband was executed by Muhammad's men in the Battle of Khaybar and she was taken prisoner. She was married to Muhammad just hours after the execution because of her high status among the Jews. Thus, she was a display of triumph and was a trophy after military victory.

Over the centuries, Muslims have tried to justify this action by saying that Muhammad gave her the honor of "marriage" as

---

[25] " Juwayriyya bint al-Harith." In The Oxford Dictionary of Islam. Ed. John L. Esposito. Oxford Islamic Studies Online. 22-Jun-2019. <http://www.oxfordislamicstudies.com/article/opr/t125/e1224>.

opposed to being a concubine and also gave her a choice to convert to Islam. There is an ancient Islamic source called "Baladhuri's ninth century *Kitab Futuh al-Buldan* ("Book of Conquests")" that offers a different view of what transpired. According to this Islamic narrative[26], after the death of Muhammad, Safiyya confessed that "Of all men, I hated the prophet the most—for he killed my husband, my brother, and my father."

It's difficult to reconcile the customary benevolent belief with a quote from the person who was taken against her will in battle, lost her freedom and lost her entire family due to the violence inflicted by the winning side.

### *Ramla bint Abi Sufyan (Umm Habiba)*
She was the daughter of a tribal chief from Mecca and was offered a proposal of marriage the same year as a peace treaty was signed between Muhammad and the warring tribe, thereby strengthening Muhammad's political alliance.

### *Maymuna bint al-Harith*
She was married after Muhammad performed a pilgrimage. It is noted that it was she who proposed to him. This was not the normal way of doing things, so it showed some social standing on

---

[26]http://library.islamweb.net/Hadith/display_hbook.php?bk_no=197&pid=125747&hid=65

Maymuna's part that she was able to initiate the marriage proposal. Even at the time of pagans, this was looked upon as extraordinary.

### *Rayhana bint Zayd*

Rayhana's story is more tragic than other women who were taken as spoils of war. She was gained in a fierce battle with the Jewish Qurayza tribe (Bani Quraiza). To ensure no one would get away, Muhammad sat and watched with his child bride Aisha while his men beheaded over 800 male captives in front of them. Rayhana's husband was one of those men,[27] Muhammad chose her because of her great beauty but due to her grief, she absolutely refused marriage and remained Jewish.[28] Unmoved, he then kept her as his concubine as a trophy and as a reminder of his Jewish conquest.[29] Muslims do not like to bring up this particular woman because the stories around her are confusing. However, the Hadith is clear about Rayhana's history, as are mentions of Aisha's accounts. When taken together, there is more than enough evidence to show that she was taken captive as one of Muhammad's women right after a bloody raid under poor circumstances.

---

[27] Lings, M. (1983) Muhammad: His Life Based on the Earliest Sources. Sira
[28] https://quranx.com/Hadith/Bukhari/USC-MSA/Volume-5/Book-59/Hadith-512/
[29] https://quranx.com/Hadith/Bukhari/USC-MSA/Volume-3/Book-39/Hadith-531/

## Maria al-Qibtiyya

Muhammad's second recorded concubine was Maria, who was a
Coptic Christian (Egyptian Christian). She was a gift from Al
Muqauqis, a governor in Egypt. She and Khadija were the only
two women to give Muhammad children. He kept her as a
concubine despite the objections of his official wives, who feared
that due to her great beauty, she would be a favorite. There are
vast accounts of her physical attributes, including her long curly
hair and perfect pale skin. Maria was the second woman to bear
Muhammad a prized son, whom they named Ibrahim. After great
celebration of the birth of a long-desired son, Ibrahim died in
childhood (some say around the age of two) in Medina.

From the women in his immediate tribe, one can see that
there was both a Jewish and a Christian presence directly around
Muhammad. From Khadija's brother Warqa to Maria the Coptic
concubine, Muhammad learned from and was influenced by the
customs of Gnostic Christianity and other cults that worshiped
Mary (mother of Jesus) in the Arabian Peninsula. These
relationships and influences would later show up in some of the
writings and traditions of Islam.

## Fatima (Daughter)

Fatima was the youngest child of Muhammad and Khadija. They
had three other girls but there is discrepancy as to whether they
were Khadija's previous daughters or if they were from the

marriage with Muhammad.[30] Whatever the case, she was the apple of his eye and held his favor. She was married to Ali (leader and the first Imam of the Shia Muslims), who became the fourth caliph in 656 AD. Fatima is still highly regarded by both Sunni and Shia Muslims for she was the sole surviving child of Muhammad.

As one might imagine, there was regular strife and jealousy between the women in this highly influential household. There were also political maneuverings between the women as they tried to gain their husband's favor. It seems that Muhammad had a stronghold on his wives and harem in life and in death. In case anyone wanted to marry his wives after he passed away, there was again an injunction and clear revelation in the Quranic verse 33:53 that says:

> "And it is not [conceivable or lawful] for you to harm the Messenger of Allah or to marry his wives after him, ever. Indeed, that would be in the sight of Allah an enormity."

How wonderful that Allah supplied an exemption clause granted only to his messenger and none other! What a special privilege indeed for him to be able to marry any woman he pleased but to deny any of his wives to those who might wish to marry them long after his death.

Several of his widows, including Aisha and his daughter Fatima often spoke publicly about Islam and were recorded for

---

[30] Walther, W. (1993). *Women in Islam*. Markus Wiener Publishing Princeton & New York. p. 108.

posterity. They served as political leaders, educators of women and as role models for behavior of the ideal Muslim woman. There is a great reverence for the wives and women of Muhammad, and they are held in high esteem throughout Muslim countries and here in the United States. There is still a gravesite for his wives in Medina that visitors acknowledge and pay special homage to, especially during the sacred time of Hajj (pilgrimage). Today, these women from Islamic history are being hailed and molded into a modern movement in Islam for education and rights of women around the world.

.

# Chapter 3

# Cultural Traditions

In 2001, TIME magazine published an article that stated:

> "For his day, the Prophet Muhammad was a feminist. The doctrine he laid out as the revealed word of God considerably improved the status of women in 7th century Arabia. In local pagan society, it was the custom to bury alive unwanted female newborns; Islam prohibited the practice. Women had been treated as possessions of their husbands; Islamic law made the education of girls a sacred duty and gave women the right to own and inherit property. Muhammad even decreed that sexual satisfaction was a woman's entitlement."

The factual truth is that Muhammad helped the status of women during the pagan times and his belief in following one God was a direct departure from what the society dictated. Pagans in Arabia included those practices listed in the article as a form of idol worship, mixed with a desire to have sons to increase their family's wealth and power. However, much of Islam's policies on women began and ended in the 7th century. The Arab culture

today firmly clings to the ancient tribal structure along with
recognition of the father of the family as the patriarch and
authoritarian. The women in a traditional Arab and Muslim
family are subject to all the patriarch's actions and to restrictions,
including education, finances, marriage, along with any contact
with outsiders. The result is controlled isolation. The author of
the TIME article redeemed herself a few paragraphs later by
stating that fourteen centuries later, there hasn't been much
improvement, in fact "under Islam today, it is clear that the
religion has been used in most Muslim countries not to liberate
but to entrench inequality."[31]

When I was a Muslim, I was invariably asked by American
women about the status of women in Islam. I would always give
a similar robotic response as the author above. I would tell people
that Muhammad was ahead of his time. He prohibited female
infanticide which was a pagan custom (where instead of aborting
a child in the womb, women would give birth and then bury the
living unwanted child in the desert sand while their tribe moved
to a different location). There are Bedouin stories about how the
cries of buried infants used to haunt the mothers who practiced
this tradition. Muhammad banned this practice and said that
children were a blessing from Allah - even female children.
Surah an Nahl (The Bees in Arabic) addressed this pagan custom:

---

[31] Beyer, L. (2001). "The Women in Islam." TIME Magazine.
http://content.time.com/time/world/article/0,8599,185647,00.html

"And when the news of [the birth of] a female [child] is brought to any of them, his face becomes dark, and he is filled with inward grief! He hides himself from the people because of the evil of that whereof he has been informed. Shall he keep her with dishonor or bury her in the earth? Certainly, evil is their decision" (Quran 16:58 & 59).

This tradition was played out in my life when my aunt came crying out of the delivery room with news that my mother had given birth to a third daughter. She was visibly upset and thought that my father (who has no sons) would have been terribly upset. My father simply told her in front of me that it was Allah's will and that all children (girls or boys) were a blessing from heaven. Still today, Muslims believe that the Quran is unclear on its stance for abortion. There is debate today that affects modern Muslim women who wish to abort their children and are unclear on rulings from the Quran due to confusing language. An article from the Muslim Institute titled "The future of abortion rights in Islam"[32] shares the frustration of what is a proper ruling on the matter. However, the Muslim Brotherhood published a statement[33] to clarify Islamic ruling by stating:

"A closer look at these articles reveals what decadence awaits our world, if we sign this document:
1. Granting girls full sexual freedom, as well as the freedom to decide their own gender and the gender of their partners (ie, choose to have normal or homo- sexual relationships), while raising the age of marriage.

---

[32] Shameen, N. (2013). "The future of abortion rights in Islam" https://musliminstitute.org/freethinking/islam/future-abortion-rights-islam
[33] March 14, 2013. Muslim Brotherhood Official Statement. http://ikhwanweb.com/muslim-brotherhood-statement-denouncing-un-women-declaration-for-violating-sharia-principles/

2. Providing contraceptives for adolescent girls and training them to use those, while legalizing abortion to get rid of unwanted pregnancies, in the name of sexual and reproductive rights.
3. Granting equal rights to adulterous wives and illegitimate sons resulting from adulterous relationships.
4. Granting equal rights to homosexuals and providing protection and respect for prostitutes.
5. Giving wives full rights to file legal complaints against husbands accusing them of rape or sexual harassment, obliging competent authorities to deal husbands punishments similar to those prescribed for raping or sexually harassing a stranger.
6. Equal inheritance (between men and women).
7. Replacing guardianship with partnership, and full sharing of roles within the family between men and women such as: spending, child care and home chores.
8. Full equality in marriage legislation such as: allowing Muslim women to marry non-Muslim men, and abolition of polygamy, dowry, men taking charge of family spending, etc.
9. Removing the authority of divorce from husbands and placing it in the hands of judges and sharing all property after divorce.
10. Cancelling the need for a husband's consent in matters like: travel, work, or use of contraception.
These are destructive tools meant to undermine the family as an important institution; they would subvert the entire society and drag it to pre-Islamic ignorance."

The Muslim Brotherhood further encouraged all women's organizations, the leaders of Muslim countries and their United Nations representatives to reject and condemn these types of actions and to repent of this as an act against the standards of Islam. So, it seems that while one side is trying to cater to modern issues and women's rights, the other (and perhaps more forceful) side is saying the opposite to the Muslim world. There exists a great dichotomy that causes confusion.

In discussing traditions, I can only speak to my own experience and what life was like for an upper, middle class Muslim family from Pakistan. While we lived in the Middle Eastern countries of Saud Arabia and United Arab Emirates, we had privileges given to those who were of an educated class. My father was working as an engineer and my mother was a rarity - she was a female physician (an OBGYN) who worked outside the home in the 1960s and 1970s.

Even today, life in third world countries function with the hidden strata of the "haves" and the "have nots." There are rights and privileges given to those with an education and family blood lines. Because of my parents' education, they were valued members of society both in Pakistan and in the Middle East. Because of my mother's royal bloodlines (Mughal), we had family connections that helped to place us at a certain level of Pakistani society that granted us great freedoms.

While traditional roles of women can vary from country to country and from class to class in society, there are many similarities when it comes to living as a Muslim woman. The woman has domain only over her household and children until they become of age to study the Quran and learn their prayers. For boys and girls, that age is usually around seven or eight years old and most clerics state that children should be admonished for not memorizing their prayers by the age of ten. Around the same age, children are enrolled in madrasas (religious schools) and are under the tutelage of an Imam (or cleric – a religious leader).

Girls can also attend a madrasa to read the Quran, but after they have completed their reading, they go back under their father's protection. Females always are under the care of a male. There is a saying in the East *"A girl belongs to her father, a woman to her husband and a mother to her son."* There is no such thing as an independent life without a male figure for a woman from the cradle to the grave.

There are even guidelines about how to raise babies in the Quran and Hadith. Both have rules about nursing an infant (should nurse them until they are two years old - Quran 2:233), about circumcision, about what to do as soon as the baby is born (put something sweet in his or her mouth, like a date [Hadith Bukhari] called tahneek in Arabic), whisper the call to prayer in a newborn's ear (tradition), have a celebration called an aqeeqah (Hadith Bukhari) where the parents sacrifice two lambs for a boy and one lamb for a girl. The differences of a female's and a male's worth in a Muslim society begin at the birth of the child.

"A girl belongs to her father, a woman to her husband and a mother to her son." There is no such thing as an independent life without a male figure for a woman from the cradle to the grave.

monasabahbooks.com

**Marriage**

As mentioned in the previous chapter, Muhammad was betrothed to Aisha when she was six and he was 53 years old. In Islam, there is no minimum age for marriage to a female child. The Sunnah or tradition simply state that the marriage can be consummated when the child turns nine years of age. Just because a tradition exists does not automatically mean that all Muslim men want to marry children. Many men choose to marry women who are at least in their teenage years. My parents were married in their twenties, and my maternal grandfather married my grandmother when she was fifteen. This was more than double the age of the prophet's wife. However, the Islamic rules are valid and ready to apply in case a man has a desire to marry someone much younger.

Islamic critics argue that throughout history there were numerous marriages arranged between children. This was a standard practice throughout Europe, especially in the ranks of the nobility. The difference here however, is that Muhammad is held as a model to all Muslim men – even today in modern times. Again, Jesus never was married, nor did he condone arranged marriages, child brides or any other marital practices of the Jewish people at his time. This is not a practice for Evangelical Christians.

In the United States, child marriage is expressly forbidden. Yet, when I worked at a Fortune 500 company in California, I was invited by a fellow Muslim employee to a marriage of her

fourteen-year-old daughter to a man who was in his mid-thirties.
I was surprised because I knew her young daughter was just
starting high school. The woman told me that since the girl was
getting married, she would be taken care of and didn't need an
education, so she would not complete high school. The man was
well-established in life and would supply all her needs. The
marriage was of course, sanctioned by her parents and they were
overjoyed at the wonderful match for their daughter and they
wanted to celebrate this with the community. There are many
Muslims here in the States who would agree that Islam's practices
of early marriage are far better than dating in the West, where
young girls lose their virginity to boys or men and then are "used
up" (this was a direct quote from a Muslim woman). Even then as
a Muslim, I could not condone this practice of child marriage.
Little did I know that it was permissible in Islam and openly
practiced elsewhere. It was just a bit jarring to come face to face
with this practice in California during the 1990s.

A Muslim father's honor is directly tied to the virginal status
of his daughters. A marriage can bring title, prestige and money
into a family. It goes back to the tribal system in Saudi Arabia,
where a daughter was looked upon as a drain on the family,
unless she attracted good marriage prospects that could give the
parents some social standing in the community. Again, the same
was true for the medieval times in Europe and all over the world
as advantageous marriages helped to gain alliances for kingdoms.
The main point here is that we are living in the twenty first

century and not in 650 AD or in the dark ages, yet the ancient system of contracted marriages still exists for many Muslim families.

In my first book, "From Isa to Christ - A Muslim Woman's Search for the Hand of God," I addressed the fact that arranged marriages have been a part of our family's tradition for centuries. My great-grandparents, grandparents, uncles, aunts, parents and sibling had an arranged marriage. I was also supposed to have an arranged marriage. This is a fact that is not kept secret but is celebrated by the family from an early age. Ever since I could remember, my parents affirmed and reminded us of the fact that it is the custom in our family to have an arranged marriage. It is still considered to be a way of life in many Muslim countries and children are to accept it as an absolute command from their parents.

Moving to the United States gave me freedoms I had never experienced before. I was able to dress as I pleased (within some limits - still had to wear modest clothes) and my parents encouraged our participation and involvement in school activities. When my sibling's arranged marriage was announced one day after graduation from a professional, graduate school, I remained in shock for several months. I did not think my parents would go through with the antiquated custom since we lived in the United States.

I had heard of a girl from a Muslim family who had been able to meet her intended husband and they had been allowed to go out on "dates" (supervised, of course) with him. He had been born in the United States and was considered to be quite the catch. I secretly thought that maybe my parents would be a modern exception like this one and allow each one of us to do something a bit different. I was wrong.

Arranged marriages are not dictated by the Quran, but when taken together with the Hadith, there isn't much room left for interpretation. In her thought-provoking book "Cruel and Usual Punishment" author Nonie Darwish[34] (a former Muslim from Egypt, now convert to Christianity), showed what a marriage contract paper looks like under Sharia law. There is an actual contract that exists for both the husband and the wife to sign. The groom completes the paperwork and then it is passed on to the bride. It is startling to see three more blanks under the husband's information where he can write in the names of his wives. For a woman, the contract explicitly asks for the name of her representative and her "condition of virginity." The contract can be terminated if she is being misrepresented to her husband as a virgin. She has to not only confess her intact physical state but also sign the contract knowing that the blanks could be filled in with names of other women under Islamic law (see Chapter on Women in the East for a discussion on polygamy).

This was a threat I lived under my entire single life. I was told by my educated mother that if I had messed around with boys,

---

[34]Darwis, N. (2009). Cruel and Usual Punishment. Thomas Nelson.

they would do a physical exam before my marriage to see my state. If there was any wrongdoing, it would bring shame down upon the whole family and a terrible result for me. That threat and whether or not they were actually going to carry through with it, was enough! For this reason (and others), there is no dating allowed in the Muslim community. The whole community would police this effort and report you to the head of the family or even to the Imam at the local mosque if they even saw a woman in the company of men. An article from India Today[35] shares statistics on how many Muslim women in India do not know what is in their marriage contract. They indicated that over 75% did not know what was written in their nikah nama (marriage contract) or did not read it at all (like me) and 47% did not have possession of it to be able to read or review it at the time of the survey. In addition, 55% of the women were married before the age of 18, and in an effort to bring the laws of Islam into the twenty-first century, three-fourths of those surveyed would like to see the marriage age increased to 21 years old. These figures echo other studies I have reviewed from Iran, Pakistan, and east Asian countries. There is a clamoring for changing the way Islam looks at marriage and women's rights from the east to west. However, Islamic laws and rules (and the Quran) are self-limiting and immovable. Centuries of progress will not challenge the system.

---

[35] Datta, D. (20 Feb 2017). "The War on Women." India Today. Retrieved Online

Very few (if any) Muslim women would ever stop to read through the marriage contract. There is no doubt about the tremendous trust daughters give to their fathers. I did not even know I had a marriage contract written up, nor did I harbor any desire to see it. Peeking out from under my ornate, hand-embroidered bridal head covering, I signed somewhere on a document that was presented to me. In the state of elation about the fulfillment of my marriage to my husband, I did not bother to look to see what I had signed in actuality or if my intended's name was even written on the document! For all I know, in my ignorance and naiveté I could have signed off on a marriage to another man. In a Muslim marriage, the bride sits in another room that is partitioned off with the women of both families. Isolated this way, the bride does not see the marriage proceedings, is not involved in the discussion between the men, does not see the actual man she is marrying and is kept completely ignorant of the contract negotiations taking place in the other room. In my case, the other room was separated by a screened partition, so I could overhear male voices. I still did not know what was going on until the marriage ceremony was over and the Imam (cleric) brought out a pen for me to sign the marriage contract.

After the first signature, I was also presented a heavy, official looking ledger to sign that showed that we agreed to the Imam's terms for a Muslim marriage ceremony and that we agreed to raise our children as Muslims, as well as attend his local mosque. This was an extra step I had never heard of and I thought that maybe it was just our local mosque's custom. The book contained several columns and looked like a registry. I had to sign my name right beside my husband's signature and date of marriage. For several decades, I never saw the Islamic certificate of marriage, but while I was drafting this book, my mother gave me the original certificate (see photo) that indicates the bride price (Sadaq or Mahr) of $5000.00.

**Mona's Muslim Marriage Certificate**

There are websites that argue that the Mahr amount should not be excessively low (as to resemble the price of a prostitute – according to one website) or too high, that the woman might think she's really worth a lot to the man. There was no money exchanged or demanded during my ceremony or afterwards by either party. Even if anyone wanted payment, my intended husband was a poor college student and hardly had any money! The marriage contract is a poignant reminder of what we went through in order to be married and serves as a memory for us to share with our children.

An internet article[36] written by a woman from Pakistan, addressed the phenomenon of not knowing the contents or seeing documents during the Muslim marriage. She began the article by stating that she held two master's degrees from Columbia, yet when it came time to read the fine print on her marriage contract, she was clueless. When she asked each of her family members to at least show her what she was signing, there were frowns of disapproval, clucking at her audaciousness and virtually shutting down any further conversation about the contract. It was none of her business... literally. The marriage contract usually has monetary amounts listed for the dowry a woman brings to the marriage and the money that a man gives. It is called Haq Mahr (Haq means "right" and Mahr means "payment" or "obligatory sum") or more commonly known as the bride price.

The bride price can be whatever the groom or groom's family agrees upon. If you search Haq Mahr and bride price together, you will find several discussion groups that are asking what the going rate is these days. One website said that they heard it was

---

[36]Nasir, A..(2010). "I Should Have Read My Islamic Marriage Contract." http://www.slate.com/articles/double_x/doublex/2010/02/i_should_have_read_my_islamic_marriage_contract.html

around $10,000, only then to be repudiated by another Muslim fatwa[37] on the matter. Turns out that a fatwa states one should use the formula used by Muhammad for his wives:

> "The scholar Ibn Khaldoon said:
> 'The consensus of the scholars from the beginning of Islam and the time of the Sahaabah and the Taabi'een has been that the shar'i dirham is that of which ten coins weigh seven mithqaals of gold. The ooqiyah is forty dirhams of this type, and on this basis, it is seven-tenths of a dinar... All of these amounts are agreed upon by scholarly consensus (ijmaa').'(*Muqaddimah Ibn Khaldoon*, p. 263).
> Based on this, the weight of a dirham in grams is   2.975 grams. So the mahr of the wives of the Propet (peace and blessings of Allah be upon him) was 500x2.975 = 148.5 grams of silver. The price of one gram of pure silver that has not been worked is approximately 1 riyal, so the mahr in riyals is approximately 1487.5 riyals. In dollars it is approximately $396.70, And Allah knows best."[38]

There are cultural Muslims who would take offense to this by saying that they have given a much larger amount of Haq Mahr, because they want the bride to not want for anything. One Muslim groom even bragged that he gave the bride her own home (I guess it was apart from his own?) as a Haq Mahr. The Muslim leaders have an answer for that as well and they call that person a "fool."[39]

There are women who say with a face filled with pride that the groom's family put down one US dollar for the Haq Mahr

---

[37] Fiqh of the family - Dowry. by Sheikh Muhammed Salih Al-Munajjid. https://islamqa.info/en/3119

[38] Fiqh of the family - Dowry. by Sheikh Muhammed Salih Al-Munajjid. https://islamqa.info/en/3119

[39] https://islamqa.info/en/answers/10525/reducing-the-mahr-is-the-sunnah

because they were so pious and believed that Allah would provide for the wife. The difficult part of this contract is that the same rules do not apply to the dowry a woman brings to the marriage. If divorced, she doesn't get a good deal in the end and many times will be lucky to leave with what little she brought to the marriage.

There are still others who would argue that the Haq Mahr is simply a tradition only for show but is not akin to buying a bride. For those who take that stance, why is there a line item in a "contract?" The only conclusion I could come to was that marriage is not a love affair for Muslims. It is a business transaction.

**Veiling**

Apart from the many traditions surrounding marriage, there are other customs that the West wants to know about. Veiling is sometimes looked on as a physical separation from other American women and the media does not help the perception as they tend to equate veiling with oppression or even as having terrorist tendencies. Some of the frequent questions I am asked is on covering. Why do women veil? What does the Quran say? Why do some Muslim women wear a full veil while others are partially veiled?

Veiling is in the media spotlight today. There are Western women who are wearing a hijab as a sign of solidarity with their Muslim female friends. This is looked down upon by the Muslim women. In fact, half of the Muslim women I know are furious about Westerners putting on their customs (because they don't understand the significance) while the other half laugh about Americans adopting customs they don't understand in order to appease those who cry out for diversity.

First, the terms for covering need to be defined as they cause a great deal of confusion. The New York Times had a full article on this topic in 2016 titled "What's That You're Wearing? A Guide to Muslim Veils."[40]

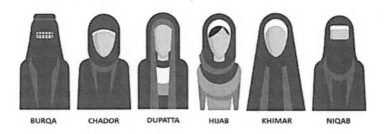

**Types of Muslim Veils**

**Abaya (Ah-buy-aah)** is a loose flowing garment that covers everything except the face, hands and feet (see also Chador). **Burqa (Boor-kah) or Burka** is what I am most familiar with, as it shows up in the Taliban restricted regions of Afghanistan and Pakistan. It covers the face & body, leaving the hands and feet uncovered. It has a heavy veil over the eyes that can either be

---

[40]Goldman, R. https://www.nytimes.com/2016/05/04/world/what-in-the-world/burqa-hijab-abaya-chador.html?_r=0

solid or perforated, like lace. They are traditionally seen in colors such as blue, black, olive green and white.

**Chador (Chah-door)** is mostly used in Iran, covers from head to toe. In Iran, black chador is the standard to wear in public but in Pakistan, vibrant colors can be seen everywhere.

**Dupatta (Doo-put-ah)** The Pakistani version of a veil a scarf or a shawl and is also called a Chador in Urdu. It's my favorite thing to wear still as a Christian - not out of any obligation, but only because I think they are beautiful and stylish. I have several of these long shawls in the traditional wool, with rich embroidery of paisley and floral designs. Women typically drape it over the head and over the shoulders in a fashionable manner. For the summer months, it makes its appearance in light cottons and even transparent chiffon

**Hijab (Hee-job)** is simply a head scarf. It can be tied tightly or worn loosely on the head. Many people refer to all veils as a hijab. The Quran uses the word hijab to mean a partition.

**Jilbab (Jill-bob)** is a head to toe covering also mentioned in the Quran. Like the Hijab, it can mean any long dress or garment that covers a woman for protection.

**Khimar (Kim-aar)** is the third item of clothing for women that is mentioned in the Quran. It is anything that will cover a woman's body to avoid the gaze of lusting men. It specifically covers body parts that might provide sexual temptation.

**Niqab (Nee-cobb)** is the actual veil for the face. It is a long piece of cloth with a slit for the eyes. Many times, the Niqab is sewn in three layers. One to cover the face (allow opening for eyes), the second layer is to cover the eyes and the third to cover the hair. A Niqab is usually worn with an Abaya in Saudi Arabia and other Muslim countries.

So why did I not use a burqa as a Muslim woman, even when I lived in a Muslim country? For the answer, we need to go to the Quran to see what it says about wearing a veil. Surah 24:31 states:

> **"And tell the believing women to reduce [some] of their vision and guard their private parts and not expose their adornment** except that which [necessarily] appears thereof and to wrap [a portion of] their head covers over their chests and not expose their adornment except to their husbands, their fathers, their husbands' fathers, their sons, their husbands' sons, their brothers, their brothers' sons, their sisters' sons, their women, that which their right hands possess, or those male attendants having no physical desire, or children who are not yet aware of the private aspects of women. And let them not stamp their feet to make known what they conceal of their adornment. And turn to Allah in repentance, all of you, O believers, that you might succeed."

Here, the word for head cover is Khimar - it is to cover a woman's chest (literally "breasts"). In Surah 33:58-59 Muhammad is commanded to ask his family members and other Muslim women to wear outer garments (Jilbab - plural form) when they go out, so that they are not accosted.

> "Those who harass believing men and believing women undeservedly, bear (on themselves) a calumny and a grievous sin. O Prophet! Enjoin your wives, your daughters, and the wives of true believers that they should cast their outer garments over their persons (when abroad): That is most

convenient, that they may be distinguished and not be
harassed."

The word **hijab** ( حجاب) in the Quran does not actually refer to
women's clothing, but pertains to the need for a physical
partition or curtain. In Muhammad's home, there was an actual
screen to separate the women from visitors to the home, as is the
case in some Muslim homes today or such as the partition used
for my wedding ceremony between the men and the women
(Surah 33:53). Hijab is also used to speak of a separation between
Allah and human beings (42:51), a partition for the righteous and
unrighteous, a screen for hearts to believe (7:46, 41:5), a barrier
between believers and unbelievers (17:45), and a curtain of
darkness (38:32).

What then, are the real guidelines to which women should
adhere? I was told by my parents that the Quran does not
specifically say to cover everything up like a burqa, but that
modesty was the key. The Muslim tradition is for women's
clothing cover up to the wrists and ankles, so a long, flowing top
with long sleeves and a pair of pants would satisfy that rule. This
is the guidance I grew up with, even when living in a Muslim
country.

What is the preoccupation of the West and media with the
veil? In Saudi Arabia (considered by many to be the heart of
Islam), covering from head to toe and wearing a head covering is
mandated by law to control a woman's sexuality and thus, it
effectively renders her a non-entity. Sharia police will arrest

those who are in public violation of this law and are known to strike women openly with their batons. There was an incident in 2002 when the Saudi religious police stopped schoolgirls who were fleeing from a fire in their building because they were not wearing a hijab or a correct dress.[41] Witnesses reported that the police even stopped the men who were trying to rescue them – as a result of this interference (due to not adhering to Islamic law), fifteen girls perished in the fire. In Iran, the hijab was once banned because it went against the modernization efforts of the Shah. Today, under strict rulers, the penalty for not veiling in public is imprisonment for ten days, up to two months per incident. What started off as a rule for separation has turned into a religion of segregation, complete with a separate entrance in most mosques for women and a separate place of prayer behind a screen, which is behind the men praying. For Hadith points out "Abu Huraira said: The best rows for men are the first rows, and the worst ones the last ones, and the best rows for women are the last ones and the worst ones for them are the first ones."[42]

If a woman was accidentally standing in front of a man, his prayer would be null and void.

"Abu Dharr reported: The Messenger of 'Allah ﷺ said: When any one of you stands for prayer and there is a thing before him equal to the back of the saddle that covers him and in case

---

[41] "Saudi police 'stopped' fire rescue". BBC. March 15, 2002.
http://news.bbc.co.uk/2/hi/middle_east/1874471.stm
[42] Sahih Muslim, Vol. 1, Book of Prayers, Hadith 881 Retrieved online
https://muflihun.com/muslim/4

> there is not before him (a thing) equal to the back of the saddle, **his prayer would be cut off by (passing of an) ass, woman, and black Dog.** I said: O Abu Dharr, what feature is there in a black dog which distinguish it from the red dog and the yellow dog? He said: O, son of my brother, I asked the Messenger of Allah ﷺ as you are asking me, and he said: The black dog is a devil."[43]

In the Hadith verses, his wife Aisha took offense to this by saying "You likened us to the asses and the dogs (Hadith 1038)."

Why is Islam so concerned with separation of women and men? Why are there barriers and obstacles raised for women to go through? There are many factors that determine the answer to those questions but most of the answers revolve around controlling female sexuality (Arabic term "awrah"). It would take too long to catalogue all the verses in the Hadith that address sexual intercourse and all the physical terms associated with it. The guidelines in Islam are written for men to be able to control just about everything under their influence to give them advantage, supremacy and ultimate authority.

There is social pressure in some countries to wear the hijab - including Muslims living in Westernized society to show their allegiance to Islam. There are other Muslims, like my family that do not cover with a veil and never really have. It is curious and confusing to me how many American women, with no Muslim background or inclination want to join in the movement to wear a

[43] Sahih Muslim, Vol. 1, Book of Prayers, Hadith 1032 Retrieved online https://muflihun.com/muslim/4

hijab or even compliment and encourage Muslims to wear their hijab.

I would like to note here that in the Bible, 1 Corinthians 11:2-10 has a section about head coverings:

> "Now I commend you because you remember me in everything and maintain the traditions even as I delivered them to you. But I want you to understand that the head of every man is Christ, the head of a wife is her husband, and the head of Christ is God. Every man who prays or prophesies with his head covered dishonors his head, but every wife who prays or prophesies with her head uncovered dishonors her head, since it is the same as if her head were shaven. For if a wife will not cover her head, then she should cut her hair short. But since it is disgraceful for a wife to cut off her hair or shave her head, let her cover her head. For a man ought not to cover his head, since he is the image and glory of God, but woman is the glory of man. For man was not made from woman, but woman from man. Neither was man created for woman, but woman for man. That is why a wife ought to have a symbol of authority on her head, because of the angels."

The way to address Scripture in the Bible is to look at the verses before and after. The portion before in 1 Corinthians 10 is about having freedom in Christ. In Corinth, the women who removed their head covering were feminists who were rising against the patriarchy and those who shaved their heads were prostitutes. In the Israelite culture, Deuteronomy 21:12 states that a shaved head for a woman indicated mourning and shame as well. Thus, Paul is addressing the order God gave us from creation and having order in the Church. It is a cultural representation of this order because women in that culture were to cover their heads in submission. On the surface, this can seem like the Bible is advocating wearing of the hijab. However, it is not a commandment to cover a woman's head but is a reminder for women to understand their role to submit to their husband as well as for the man to submit to Christ as head of the Church. The website Got Questions.com states:

> "A woman has the choice to wear a head covering if she views it as a sign of her submission to the authority of her husband. However, it is a personal choice and not something that should be used to judge spirituality. The real issue here is the heart attitude of obedience to God's authority and submission to His established order "as to the LORD" (Ephesians 5:22). God is far more concerned with an attitude of submission than an outward display of submission via a head covering.[44]"

My upbringing defines my view of the veil and covering. It was prevailed upon me by the Muslim women in my family that men were weak and could not control their sexual desires. Today, I believe that at best, this statement is an insult to all Muslim men. At worst, it is a license for men to behave badly towards women in society. I was clearly instructed that women were held responsible by Islam for making sure that we did not entice men (see Surah 24:31 quoted above) and that we alone could "guard our private parts." I was told that my hair was a temptation, my skin, my eyes and even the jewelry I wore could be a temptation to men. In 2008, Egypt heralded a national advertising campaign with two images: one was a lollipop with the wrapper intact with a subheading of "With Hijab." It showed a fly buzzing right past

---

[44] "Should Christian women wear head coverings?"
https://www.gotquestions.org/head-coverings.html

it. The other picture was an unwrapped lollipop with many flies landing upon it, subtitled "Without Hijab." The Arabic text below stated "You cannot stop them, but you can protect yourself. He who created you knows best for you." Women are shown in that society as a sweet confection, ready to be devoured by men who are like flies. I don't think either one of those comparisons are endearing. In Afghanistan and Iran, the marketing image had an additional tag line: "Hijab is not a piece of cloth on your head, it's a way of life."

I remember watching an old black and white Indian movie where a young Muslim woman was traveling to her parents' home by train. During the long journey, she grew tired and put her beautiful bare feet adorned with anklets and henna upon the empty seat next to her so she could sleep. The young hero across the aisle from her became mesmerized by her bare feet. He became entirely fixated, enticed and the camera zoomed onto his face as he started sweating profusely, and became visibly agitated while watching her sleep. When I questioned why he was sweating, I was once again told that this is why women need to cover – even the sight of my bare feet was enough to bring men into sexual temptation and this would count as haram (bad deed or sin) for me. It was entirely up to me to be modest and not cause any man undue temptation which would then cause a reaction from him, for men were weak in that nature and women could control their urges better than them.

Of course, for the logical mind the natural follow-up question is ... what about him? Isn't it haram for a Muslim man to think that way? The answer is an absolute "NO!" These rules don't apply to men - women are simply the object and the entire cause of the evil temptation (especially due to the temptation of Adam by Eve) and thus, the responsibility rests wholly upon us. The belief in an evil curse being placed on a person is also confirmed by Hadith "'A'isha reported that Allah's Messenger ﷺ commanded the use of incantation for curing the influence of an evil eye."[45] This connects directly to what Muhammad thought of women in another Hadith: "Narrated Abdullah bin 'Umar: Allah's Apostle said, "Evil omen is in the women, the house and the horse."[46] and another one in case that one wasn't clear, "Narrated Usama bin Zaid: The Prophet said, "After me I have not left any affliction more harmful to men than women."[47] Not my words but the words of the one hailed by Islam as a model for all to follow. Enough said.

---

[45] Sahih Muslim, Vol. 5, Book of Greetings, Hadith 5445 Retrieved online https://muflihun.com/muslim/26
[46] Sahih al-Bukhari Vol. 7, Book of Marriage, Hadith 30 Retrieved online https://muflihun.com/bukhari/62/30
[47] Sahih al-Bukhari Vol. 7, Book of Marriage, Hadith 33

# Chapter 4

# Muslim Women in the East

I was born in the Middle East because my parents moved there shortly after their marriage in order to earn a living - jobs were more plentiful in prosperous Arabia than in Pakistan at the time, and there, they learned to be fluent in Arabic. Some of my earliest memories were of having a picnic in the middle of the desert. We would pack up our station wagon with baskets of prepared food, plates, cutlery, tea preparations, large, plush reclining pillows and a thick, beautiful hand-woven carpet. My father would drive out to the remote desert with miles of sand dunes and park the car under some shade if he could find it. There was one particular valley we would almost always go to. I loved it because there were vast areas to run and hills to climb.

The hand-knotted rug would ceremoniously be spread out on sand, the signal to all that the picnic had begun! As the little children jumped off the boulders, ran, and danced around the designated area, the women would get the food set up in order to eat. It was a feast that lasted all day long and most definitely an affair to remember. This was only one of the many Saudi customs that is still endearing to me. The culture is so rich with hospitality and warmth but there was a definite undercurrent of restriction I perceived, even as a child.

I lived amidst the strict Arabs until I was moved to Pakistan with my nanny and older sister. This was where all our family and distant relatives lived. In Pakistan, there seemed to be a collective breath of relief from the pressures of the uncompromising Muslim life in Arabia. There was a noticeable relaxing of rules in the house and in social places. Outside the home, women wore colorful clothing instead of the black hijab that was common to Arabia. There were other differences in everyday life, interaction and pace that I discovered between the two Muslim nations even at an early age.

I started school in Pakistan (that was the reason for my move back and transition) and was immersed in the culture immediately. I did not speak the language at that time. I only spoke a little Arabic and English (my parents taught us English at home). When I began learning Urdu, my Arabic was quickly forgotten. I went to the Islamabad School for Girls, which was run by all women. These women were educated and willing to teach other girls to achieve a higher station in life. Islamabad is the capital of Pakistan and a bustling city, so the school had many families that were well to do - especially for a public school.

Pakistan used to be a part of India until 1947, when it won its independence. Because of its close association with India, the customs remain the same. Pakistan has more in common with India than it does with the Middle Eastern countries. This presents a problem for the Muslim Pakistanis, as the hidden desire of every Muslim is to be close to the Arabs - just like the prophet of Islam.

There are issues that can arise from having a tradition and culture that resembles more of the polytheistic India than the Islamic Arabia. For example, in Saudi Arabia, the marriage customs mimic the desert people's traditions. There is a formality associated with the service and a great solemnity. In Pakistan, the celebration of marriage is a week-long party, full of vivacious colors, music and dancing. Henna is applied in intricate patterns on the women's skin (Indian custom for fertility, but done mostly for decoration by Muslims), along with the rich green and deep mustard yellow colors of fresh spices. In Saudi Arabia, the bride wears white or a light color. The color is not dictated in Islam but is rather a custom of the country or region. In Asian countries, the brides usually wear red – the color for luck. This includes India, Pakistan, Indonesia, China, and Japan, among other countries. Again, the color of the bride's finery is a tradition that has nothing to do with religion.

When you ask an American what they know about Muslim women, there is a standard answer: they are oppressed, veiled under a hijab and kept ignorant. When I speak about my life, they are surprised at the flexibility I had in modern clothing as an American Muslim woman. My parents allowed their daughters to wear modest clothing outside the home. No shorts, no tank tops, nothing that showed too much skin. This is what I was taught as a girl - that the world will look at you as a sexual object and it is up to you to protect yourself from predators who want to use and abuse you. So, they instructed us to cover up, dress modestly, stay away from boys and all will be well. These are good rules to live by even as a Christian woman, especially in a world that sends out all the wrong signals about a woman's worth being represented by her physical assets or by the opposite sex.

The media doesn't help Muslim or Christian women by telling both of us that we need to pay for self-improvement because we are lacking when compared to people around us. In this type of a world that doesn't know whether to be offended at modesty or applaud it, at least Islam presents a clear message to women: cover up. The rules my parents set for me helped me to understand that I could be valued for my achievements, education and not for the amount of skin I showed. These are the same guidelines for clothing and behavior that I passed on to my children: dress modestly, act kindly and walk humbly with the Lord.

## Community – The Ummah

Typically, Muslim countries are fairly homogenous in diversity and in religion. For example, Indonesia is mostly made up of Asians who are Muslim (almost 90%) with a small scattering of Christians. Same is true in Pakistan, except the Muslims make up about 98%. Women there worship together, eat together, fast together and live in smaller communities together. The result is very strong familial and community ties. It is not uncommon to find families and extended families living within a few square miles of one another. In the villages, life takes on even a greater proximity as they share familial names, inter-marry and share land, as well as centuries of traditions.

In Saudi Arabia, women do not venture out much due to the high desert temperatures during the day. Recently, I had a friend who told me that her American husband (who traveled to Saudi Arabia for work) noticed that there were no women outdoors at all. They seemed to be entirely missing from society. As a norm, many women do not work outside the home in Saudi Arabia. When we lived there, our neighbors and friends stayed mainly indoors but my mother (always being an exception to the rule) worked full-time at the hospital. Some have servants who do the errands, go grocery shopping and other tasks. This leaves women to join together in homes and establish friendships and close ties as their children play together.

When one adds multiple marriages to the mix, the results can be even more complicated and can cause family issues in the

home, including birth order, birth right and inheritance. As in
Muhammad's case, wives can develop jealousy and strife. Of
course, being a culture that is fueled by the dueling code of
honor/shame, the average person would never be permitted to see
the discord within the home. Outside the house, all is well. The
children will get along and the wives would never even hint at
anything that could bring dishonor to the family name.

There have been several books written about the ultra-
wealthy royal family of Saudi Arabia where the reader gets an
intimate look at the secluded life behind the veil. There are
stories of modern-day harems, multiple marriages, child brides,
alcoholism and abuse. When I had heard of a particular book
coming out in the 1990's I was told expressly by my mother that
they were lies that the infidel was spreading through American
media and that I was forbidden to read it. Of course, that only
heightened my interest and left me wondering what I was
missing.

The lifestyles of the wealthy and the middle class are
different than the lower working classes. In other popular books
about the villages in Afghanistan, there is insight from Non-
Government Organizations (NGOs) that shed some light into
what transpires there today. There are rough living conditions,
with multiple families crouching under thatched mud roofs. The
poor in these countries have next to nothing. Homes may have
only a small open flame burner in the corner where the family
does all their cooking and water has to be brought in from the

village well. This is evident in India, Pakistan, Afghanistan, and other third world countries throughout Africa and Asia- this is not just limited to Muslim families. These NGOs brought aid to struggling Islamic nations and they also brought attention to hidden secrets in the Muslim world, such as Female Genital Mutilation (FGM).

**Female Genital Mutilation (FGM)**

The Detroit Free Press published an article in April 2017 about three female Muslim doctors who were arrested in Detroit, Michigan for mutilating six to nine-year-old girls. Included in the arrests was a female physician named Dr. Nagarwala. There is an 11-page report from the Department of Justice[48] from April 13, 2017 from the Emergency Room Physician. It was reported on another website[49] that "Dr. Nagarwala's attorney, Shannon Smith, claimed in her initial court hearing that no cutting of the seven-year-old alleged victims took place and that excess skin was simply scrapped off to be buried in a religious ceremony. The Free Press, however, reported that documents they reviewed showed the injuries to the two Minnesota girls' genitals were "much more severe" than Nagarwala is claiming." This was an eye-opening report that uncovered a truth hidden under the

---

[48] https://www.justice.gov/opa/pr/detroit-emergency-room-doctor-arrested-and-charged-performing-female-genital-mutilation
[49] https://gellerreport.com/2017/04/report-detroit-muslim-fgm-doctor-mutilated-girls-far-worse-admits.html/#comment-953669

private life of a practicing Muslim. This was normally a practice found in Islamic countries in Africa, but the report found that there are Western countries with Muslims who are practicing the act here today. For example, it was reported that in Manchester, England there were almost 2000 Muslim girls that had undergone FGM.

Many Muslims will correctly tell you (including me, when I was a Muslim!) that this is not a normal thing practiced by all Muslims. However, one should know that the Hadith (traditions and guidelines for Muslims to use) **does not forbid it.** Something that was culturally practiced mainly in Africa was now spreading to other countries in Asia.

A study done by WADI (a German-Austrian NGO) in 2003 revealed that the FGM was not just limited to the African continent. After a year of medical work from all-female teams in Kurdistan, the workers began to gain trust with the local women. Soon, they found that close to sixty percent of the women had undergone cutting.[50] While many Muslims will deny that Islam has a link to FGM, there is no denying the fact that the countries in which it is practiced are all indeed Muslim.

The most often mentioned narration reports a debate between Muhammad and Um Habibah (or Um 'Atiyyah). This woman, known as an exciser of female slaves, was one of a group of

---

[50] http://www.meforum.org/1629/is-female-genital-mutilation-an-islamic-problem

women who had immigrated with Muhammad. Having seen her, Muhammad asked her if she kept practicing her profession. She answered affirmatively, adding:

> "...unless it is forbidden, and you order me to stop doing it."
> Muhammad replied: "Yes, it is allowed. Come closer so I can teach
> you: if you cut, do not overdo it, because it brings more radiance to
> the face, and it is more pleasant for the husband."[51]

That quote and story state that Muhammad allowed it and praised the act of female circumcision as something that improves sexual relations in a marriage. Since Muhammad's example is held up as a model for Muslim society, so are his sayings. Abu Sahlieh further cited Muhammad as saying, "Circumcision is a *sunna* (tradition) for the men and *makruma* (honorable deed) for the women." In order to be clear, the Quran does not make mention of it, only Hadith and even in the Hadith, it is not forbidden, but only offers a warning to not cut severely. Now, what exactly entails as "cutting severely" may be open for interpretation by the person performing the act. Again, there are fatwas (Islamic decrees like Fatwa 60314)[52] that address this issue.

No one wants to talk about this in Islamic society, especially in modern times. Why? It is an enormous taboo that's combined with the **honor/shame culture**. Islam has its roots in the Eastern mentality that honor of the family should come before anything

---

[51] https://islamqa.info/en/60314
[52] http://www.webcitation.org/query?url=http://www.islam-qa.com/en/ref/60314/female_circumcision&date=2013-05-24

or anyone else. It is a culture that forbids women to be seen with or to interact with men who are not family, including doctors. This makes it more difficult to speak about personal female matters to outsiders – adding yet another barrier for the discussion of intensely private mutilation practices that have caused physical and mental pain for generations. This topic of conversation is just now coming to light as more and more Westerners are going over to historically closed Islamic nations to help in post-war efforts.

Personally, I compare the hidden tradition to hazing in college. In universities across the United States, students who were traumatized as freshmen turn around and do the very same to others as they move up the ranks into upper classmen. Examples of this can usually be found in drinking alcohol to toxic levels and other rituals in clubs, teams or organizations. Just because older women went through this trauma, they sometimes subject the young Muslim girls. Some have died from this practice because of back alley circumcisions, trauma, infection or loss of blood.

When I speak and teach about Islam and how to build a bridge with Muslims, I am inevitably asked about FGM and whether or not I had experienced this practice. I can thankfully say that Pakistan is shown on the FGM map as a country of "rare occurrence." This is not something Pakistanis would even speak about within their families (my mother practiced in both Saudi Arabia and Pakistan- I never heard her mention this in my life).

The first time I ever heard about this practice was in college and I thought it was ridiculous that such a claim was being made out of efforts to slander Islam, since I had no personal knowledge of it. I was incredibly ignorant of what was being practiced in the world.  It seems like I wasn't the only one who was ignorant. There were many others around the world who were ignorant of this going on… it took the WADI[53] report to bring it to the 21st century. Updates were given in 2010 by the Human Rights Watch that yes, indeed this is not just limited to Africa, but is prevalent in Kurdistan and no one reports it due to "embarrassment."

Even living in freedom of the United States as a citizen, many Muslim women do not speak up about divorce, domestic violence abuse, or FGM. It's simply not done, and the community believes it is so much better to leave these things in the dark where they belong. It brings great shame upon the household and the family name. The **honor/shame** culture also has overarching themes to consider such as: relationships/reputation, guilt/innocence, loyalty/disloyalty and all are seen by the community as an overall rejection of Islam. As a Muslim woman, you will be looked upon as someone who is out of control and needs to be brought back in line by the family or by the whole community.

It brings to mind a verse in the Bible from the book of Ephesians 5:13-15 "But everything exposed by the light becomes

---

[53] The Campaign Against Female Genital Mutilation. June 3, 2017. https://wadi-online.org/2017/03/06/the-campaign-against-female-genital-mutilation/

visible, for everything that is illuminated becomes a light itself. So, it is said: "Wake up, O' sleeper, rise up from the dead, and Christ will shine on you." This is an area that causes me deep sorrow - to know that these abuses are going on in the world and people are allowing little girls to be cut, traumatized and mutilated all under the guise of a religious tradition to be seen as more pious.

## Polygamy

Several Muslim websites claim that polygamy is an area that Christians and the West like to attack. Comments from authors went as far as to call it "Islam-bashing." One website in particular wanted to set the record straight to show how the rules of Islam apply to this controversial topic. Here is a long, but direct excerpt from that website:

"From His signs is that He has created for you spouses from yourselves so that you may get peace [and tranquility] through them; and He placed between you love and mercy. In these are signs for the people who reflect." (Surah ar-Room, 30:21)
"Al-Islam on Monogamy & Polygyny
Generally speaking, there are two types of marriages in Islam:
• Monogamy: one man married to one woman;
• Limited polygyny [a kind of polygamy- The term "polygyny" is preferred because polygamy means multiple spouse (one husband and multiple wives or one wife and multiple husbands) whereas polygyny only refers to marriage of one man to multiple women.]: one man married to two, three or at the most four wives. In Islam, the ideal marriage is the monogamous form of marriage. Limited polygyny is a provision approved by Islam for exceptional circumstances only; and that also with many stringent conditions (Murtaza Mutahhari, The Rights of Women in Islam published by WOFIS, Tehran). Vast majority

of Muslim men are monogamous in their marriage
relationships; those who have more than one wife are very few,
probably less than zero-point one percent of the Muslim
world…

Lamech, the grandson of Adam, had two wives.
Abraham had two wives: Sarah & Hajar.
Jacob had two wives & two concubines:
The Twelve of Tribes of Israel are from these four ladies.
David had many wives. "[54]

In order to tackle this complex topic, we need to start at the
top verse. The Quran allows multiple marriages for a man. If you
note - the verse says "spouses" as a plural. This is also stated as a
sign from Allah for people to gain peace and tranquility. There is
no special circumstance established in the Quran for a man
against taking multiple wives. The only restriction is that he
should have no more than four wives (even though as was
mentioned earlier in the book that Muhammad himself had
upwards of 11 wives and multiple concubines). The Islamic
website further goes on to "Christian-bash" (my own words and
opinion) by quoting multiple marriages from the time of Adam
(they quote Lamech as a descendant of Adam) to David.

It's too bad they stopped there and didn't pursue the point any
further. The more impressive number of wives and concubines
belongs to King David's son, Solomon at over one thousand
women in his harem. The huge departure from God's intended
design of one man and one woman (in Genesis) resulted in

[54] https://www.al-islam.org/articles/concept-polygamy-and-prophets-marriages-sayyid-muhammad-rizvi

Solomon being led away from God Almighty and into pagan practices of some of his wives. Thus he incurred God's anger, judgment and a division of his kingdom after his death.

As stated previously, Christianity does not endorse polygamy. Jesus was not married, never promoted polygamy, nor did He tell His disciples to have more than one wife. In Genesis, the Lord God set His example for all humanity by creating Eve for Adam. Only one wife for one man. Everything after that relationship denotes the sin of mankind, evident after the Fall of Adam. In other words, polygamy is not a part of God's original design for His creation. That is man's warped desire to do that which goes against God.

Abraham, the prophet who is held up as an ideal by Jews, Christians and Muslims acted against what God had willed for him. In Genesis 15, God made a one-sided covenant with Abraham and promised him countless offspring like the number of starts in the heavens. The impatience of man is seen in the very next chapter where his wife Sarah did not believe God would keep His promise and took matters into her own hands. Sarah asked Abraham to sleep with her maidservant Hagar who immediately conceived a son. As an immediate result, Sarah felt slighted and jealous. In her rage, she "dealt harshly" with Hagar. She banished Hagar to the desert wilderness. In Genesis 16:10-12, an angel of the Lord told Hagar to return and submit to her mistress. God then made Hagar a parallel promise also that " "I will surely multiply your offspring so that they cannot be numbered for multitude." She was instructed to name the child "Ishmael" which means "God listens" in Hebrew. The angel further set a course in action by telling Hagar of Ishmael's character "He shall be a wild donkey of a man, his hand against everyone and everyone's hand against him, and he shall dwell over against all his kinsmen." This not only applied to Ishmael himself but can be seen in the Old Testament scriptures as true for Ishmaelites. Ishmaelites also encompassed the Midianites who lived in the Arabian desert and were slave traders.[55]

Genesis 18 shows the patience of God as the Lord appears to Abraham and his barren wife Sarah and tells them that He will return next year when Sarah will bear a son. This promise seemed ludicrous to Sarah since they both were of an advanced age.

> "Now Abraham and Sarah were old, advanced in years. The way of women had ceased to be with Sarah. So, Sarah laughed to herself, saying, 'After I am worn out, and my lord is old, shall I have pleasure?'" (Genesis 18:11-12). Exactly as the Lord had promised, Sarah bears a son and names him Isaac which means "He laughs." For Sarah said, "God has made laughter for me; everyone who hears will laugh over me" (Genesis 21:6).

The problems for Abraham were not over yet. Just because God kept His promise did not mean that there weren't consequences for Abraham for listening to Sarah and having sexual relations with Hagar. Again, there was strife in the household between the women and Sarah turned against Hagar,

---

[55] https://www.gotquestions.org/Ishmaelites.html

asking Abraham to send her away for she refused to share the home with another woman. Sadly, Abraham took her and Ishmael to the wilderness and leaves them there. God showed His mercy again to Hagar and allowed her to remember His promise to make Ishmael into a great nation. Hagar and Ishmael settled in the wilderness of Paran and later he took a wife from Egypt.

There is a rich history in these passages that help to explain present day politics in the Middle East between Muslims and Jews. Jews hail from Isaac - the promised son of Abraham, while many Arabs and Muslims claim ancestry through Abraham's son Ishmael. There are many authors who absolutely denounce the claim Muslims make about their origins from Abraham's line. Personally, I cannot help but think about God knowing the character of Ishmael and how his hand would be against everyone, with everyone's hand against him. My upbringing as a former Muslim also has Abraham's name deeply ingrained into the prayers and beliefs of all Muslims. Hagar's desperate search for water is depicted in one of the traditions of Hajj, the annual pilgrimage to Mecca. Abraham's sacrifice of obedience is celebrated at the end of Ramadan annually by millions of Muslims.

The background on Abraham's polygamy is presented here in order to show how a prophet who was obedient to the Lord strayed and took matters into his own hands. He took another woman into the household and created havoc - not just for himself but also for future generations. When Muslims bring other accounts from the Bible into the conversation about polygamy, it is important to reiterate that polygamy is not dictated or approved by the Bible or in any Christian teaching. It opposes God's plan for marriage in the account of creation in Genesis.

I grew up believing that polygamy existed in Islam so that a man could equitably and fairly take care of multiple women in his life. This was given to me as a better system than what's evident in the Western world where men have illegitimate children through adulterous affairs (no adultery for a Muslim man, since he could claim another woman as his wife), no dating and premarital sex needed since men could marry more than one woman and take her to bed, and no broken marriages due to divorce. I was told that there was no need for divorce, since the man just kept his other wife while taking another and another. It was argued that this presented a better approach to keep the husband accountable towards his wives and the children never had to worry about divorce or having the family fall apart. Muhammad is again held up as a paragon because he rescued several women from widowhood by marriage into his household (never mind that he ordered the killing of a couple of those women's husbands before he took them as wives).

In Chapter Two, I mentioned that some of the marriage contracts have only one line for the husband to fill out his name and four blanks for the additional wives he may claim during his lifetime. There are wealthy Muslim families where the men keep the fourth line blank, only to fill it with what is a phenomenon called "weekend wife" or a temporary marriage (nikah mut'ah). They claim a wife for the weekend, verbally tell her that they divorce her three times and the next weekend, go and play with another woman's virtue for pleasure. This is not the norm - please understand I am not trying to present this as something that occurs daily.

My objective is to inform the reader that this is a loop hole in a law that allows men freedoms that women could never attain. There is a BBC article[56] titled "I do...for now - UK Muslims revive temporary marriages" in 2013 that addresses the practice of a temporary marriage and how even within the Muslim world, both Sunni and Shi'a are at odds about the practice. The article also has a video of a thirty-year-old woman who states that she wanted to have a temporary marriage along with a contract and a price that her intended had to pay. Many Muslim women vehemently protest this practice and liken it to prostitution since there is an exchange of money or goods in the form of a gift and also there is a limited time of a day, week or months associated with the contract.

During Muhammad's time, marriage to more than one woman was already an established cultural practice. There was no need to divorce the first wife in order to marry another woman because

---

[56] Mahmood, S and Nye, C. (2013). "I do... for now..." http://www.bbc.com/news/uk-22354201

the husband was socially allowed to take multiple wives, concubines and female slaves. The society saw an increase in the man's social status along with the number of women in his household and the substantial number of children. As in Muhammad's own household, there was a hierarchy set by the number of wives (the first wife always reigns at the start, but in his case, his first wife died), the favorite, the youngest, the one with the most sons, etc. Most times, the youngest or most recent wife is granted greater access to the husband, along with a larger financial gift. There is a definite pecking order and the harem creates its own sense of politics.

There is a fantastic series called "Magnificent Century" written by Meral Okay and Yılmaz Şahin that depicts Sultan Suleyman the Magnificent, King of the Ottoman Empire during the early 1500's. The lush epic Turkish drama caught my attention and curiosity because it showed the inner workings of the Muslim harem and the King dealing with multiple wives, concubines and other women in his harem. The series was, of course based upon a historical fiction. However, even though the fictional elements were present, there was a lot of truth in the way the women showed jealousy, frustration, competition and love for their one husband who provided lavishly for their physical needs.

In a situation where there is a man who is financially able to provide for multiple wives, there can be relative complacency in the household, but in lower-income families, this can be a disaster. For the Bedouin women in Arabia, a polygamous household is the norm. "Due to their lower social status, they are unlikely to initiate divorce proceedings, both for fear of losing custody of their children and because the severe social stigma that is imposed on a divorced woman is magnified if she initiates the divorce."[57] With each woman that comes into the household as a wife, the ones preceding her suffer a significant deterioration of their finances, physical and emotional abandonment. This emotional burden is not isolated, as it trickles down to that wife's children. They also fall down lower in the household ranks and as a result, even the servants know who holds most favor in the family.

Muslims who are familiar with the Old Testament might refute these claims again with those in the Bible. As mentioned earlier in the chapter, polygamy was not just a Muslim custom. It does appear in the Old Testament but was not sanctioned by God. The story of Hannah in 1 Samuel shows the competition and heartache caused by having multiple wives, especially if one was barren. These are real concerns for Muslims today.

I was faced with the notion of Muslim polygamy right here in the United States. Our Muslim community in California had a number of affluent, professional families that came from the upper echelon of society. Many were doctors, lawyers, dentists

---

[57] Einat A, Income Support for the Alternative Family - Polygamous Families as a case study, Studies in Gender and Fmnizim, Nevo Publishing Ltd., Tss"z 2007, pp. 617, 631-332

and business owners who sent their children to private schools and to top Universities. They were not the ignorant or illiterate people that the media tries to depict in their coverage. My community had women who covered with hijab and women who dressed in designer suits without a head covering. I didn't think for a second that polygamy would be a part of this elite community.

One day, while visiting a wonderful cultural Muslim family, I was introduced to one of my friend's "cousin." Later, I heard that the boy was not her cousin but was a half-brother from her father's first wife. Disturbed by this rumor, I ran to my mom who confirmed that it was not a rumor but was true. She told me not to say anything, especially to Americans as they would never understand the situation. This is where the entire situation stayed - under cover, concealed and addressed in hushed whispers during conversations within the community.

We were not allowed to talk about the second marriage nor did my parents wish to discuss the matter further. They simply shrugged their shoulders and said, "it happens." In fact, I found out later as I grew older, that some of the men within our community had multiple wives in Pakistan and other countries. That the wife we saw them with regularly was their latest one or maybe just the wife in America. An article written in 2008 by

NPR[58] estimates about 50,000 to 100,000 Muslims who engage in polygamy in the United States today. Since laws in the United States forbid polygamy, it would be difficult to know exact numbers of Muslims here who have multiple marriages with women not only in the United States, but also abroad.

I encountered another situation dealing with polygamy in the United States among Muslims after I had become a Christian. I received a phone call from a former Pastor who had been witnessing to a college girl. She had become a Christian only months before she met a charming student from Pakistan. Within months, he proposed marriage to her. She was head over heels in love with him and was getting ready to be whisked away into matrimony when the Pastor had the insight to ask her about multiple marriages for the man, since he was visiting on a student visa to study at the local University. She asked her fiancée who truthfully told her that his family would never recognize a marriage here in the United States with her was already married to a woman back at home.

The girl told me she was crushed when she found out... but to my shock, was still contemplating a marriage to this man. After getting over my concern at the proposed arrangement, I asked her why. She said that he was bound by his religion to provide for her from now until her death. She also said that he told her that she

---

[58]Hagerty, B. (2008) "Some Muslims in the U.S. Quietly Engage in Polygamy. https://www.npr.org/templates/story/story.php?storyId=90857818

would be his wife whenever he visited the United States (but that she could never come with him to Pakistan where his other wife was living). The two wives would have to stay apart in separate households and that, she was convinced, was a good thing. He convinced her that he would never humiliate her with the other wife, and she would never be in direct competition with her and her children. He also gave her complete assurance that she would never have to worry about finances -- ever.

The warped situation is still beyond my comprehension. I was able to share with her that in Christianity, God designed marriage to be between one man and one woman. Anything other than that was a system created by man for his own enjoyment. She sadly shook her head and said that she would indeed, marry him and accept his terms because she did not want to be alone. It still haunts me that such a lovely woman would have such a low sense of self and would not see herself as one created in the image of God. She was worth a lot more to the Creator God than what this man was willing to "pay" for keeping her as a wife of secondary status. Her desire for a sham marriage to a man who would not solely commit to her and would rule over her was preferable than being alone. I prayed for her to not go through with the marriage, but I do not know what happened to her after our conversation.

While polygamy is sanctioned by the Quran, not all Muslim men have multiple wives. Growing up, my father used to tease my mom that he would get another wife. Being a girl, I did not find that to be humorous at all. I saw it instead as a threat. My

mother, however took all things in stride. I especially recall one
day after we had moved to the United States when my parents
were having a small disagreement about something. My dad did
his usual teasing and said, "if you keep that up, I will go get
another wife from Pakistan." My mother was in the kitchen,
cooking. She stopped what she was doing, put her hand on her
hip and in a loud voice declared "Go ahead! In fact, I dare you.
Why don't you make sure your new wife is very young, so I can
put her to work here in the kitchen and have her cook for you
instead of me doing everything? I am still the first wife and I
would still have power over her." With that rebuttal to his
remark, he stared at her and then quietly walked away. That was
the last time I ever heard my father make that remark again.

We have many family friends here in the United States who
are Muslim, and they have had long-lasting, monogamous
marriages. The husbands are loving, caring providers who want
to protect their families and have means to educate their wives
and daughters. Not all Muslims fit into this category and it would
be a grievous error to assume that this applies to everyone.

**Divorce**

One day, over a casual lunch with Muslim friends, they began
to talk about a particular woman who had now remarried after
divorce to another Muslim man. Thus, a discussion about
divorce, women's rights and Islam came up. Tempers can flare
easily, and this was no exception. There were passionate claims

being made about how wonderful Islam was and how much women gained from the Quranic laws, while everyone nodded their heads in agreement. Someone even made the comment that the Quran does not have any sayings about divorce, but that the divorce decrees and rules are all made by the Imams. They make the point that Islam does not forbid women to divorce and that it gave women tons of rights.

I tried to sit in silence, but sometimes the unsubstantiated claims become too much to bear. I prayed quickly ("Lord Jesus, help me!") and then said that I agreed that Muhammad put an end to female infanticide (killing baby girls because of the patriarchal society and Arab desire to have only boys to carry on their family name) but apart from that... nothing more. That's when the whole table jumped on me. There were vigorous claims being made that Islam allows for women to freely divorce (no, not true) and that women do have a choice when it comes to marriage (again, not always according to the Quran). Another claim was that the "I Divorce You" statement said three times by a man to quickly divorce his wife was also not in the Quran (yes, it is... see Al Baqarah verse 2:229-230). When I challenged that the Quran does indeed have rules about women and divorce, I was told "You don't know. You read the English translation of the Quran - in Arabic, it's different." It is very convenient to blame things on the translation.

There is an entire Surah (Chapter) called "Al Talaq," which literally means divorce in Arabic. The very first verse says:

"O Prophet, when you [Muslims] divorce women, divorce them for [the commencement of] their waiting period and keep count of the waiting period, and fear Allah, your Lord. Do not turn them out of their [husbands'] houses, nor should they [themselves] leave [during that period] unless they are committing a clear immorality. And those are the limits [set by] Allah. And whoever transgresses the limits of Allah has certainly wronged himself. You know not; perhaps Allah will bring about after that a [different] matter. (Al Talaq, 65:1)."

The questions that come to mind immediately are: What is "the waiting period?" What is "clear immorality?" Notice, that the husband doesn't let them go and neither can they go of their own choice. If they leave of their own accord, it is clear immorality! It's a catch 22. A group of women I know tried to help a Muslim woman leave her husband's home because she was physically abused since the day they were married. She has suffered this way for the last twelve years. I met her six years ago, when the ladies from a church offered her a safe home. She told me then that she had no choice but to return to him, since she was his property and rightfully belonged to him. She also said that many from the Muslim community came to her and told her that she would be a pariah if she left her husband who was a successful businessman. Now, six years later, the beatings have doubled as she remains in that home with two abusers, since her son is older and is following what his father taught him. When there is a threat hanging over a woman's head that she might be replaced with another woman or be divorced in a shameful way, some women choose to stay due to these desperate circumstances.

It's interesting that even Muhammad realized how deep the bonds of marriage between one man and one woman could be. While he asked his own adopted son Zayd to divorce his own wife (so Muhammad could marry her), Muhammad would not allow his son-in-law Ali to have more than one wife, because an extra woman would hurt Muhammad's only living daughter, Fatima (emphasis mine).

> "The Hadith states "Miswar b. Makhramali reported that he heard Allah's Messenger ﷺ say, as he sat on the pulpit: The sons of Hisham b. Mughira have asked my permission to marry their daughter with 'Ali b. Abi Talib (that refers to the daughter of Abu Jahl for whom 'All had sent a proposal for marriage). But I would not allow them, I would not allow them, I would not allow them (and the only alternative possible is) that 'Ali should divorce my daughter (and then marry their daughter), **for my daughter is part of me. He who disturbs her in fact disturbs me and he who offends her offends me.**"[59]

Even though the Hadith shows how painful and harmful polygamy can be for women, he continued to practice it and allowed it for all Muslim men. Multiple wives mean multiple children and multiple children means growth for Islam.

There are specific guidelines given that allow women to ask for a divorce and the Hadith has delineated these circumstances: impotency (child bearing is extremely important), not taking care of her, and insanity. Any kind of abuse is not a valid reason: emotional, verbal or physical and this reason is dismissed in Sharia courts. In settlement of these divorces initiated by women,

---

[59] Sahih Muslim Vol. 6, Book of the Merits of the Companions, Hadith 5999 Retrieved online https://muflihun.com/muslim/31/5999

there is usually a request for the bride price to be repaid by the
husband to the bride or to her male family members who were
witnesses to the marriage (Mahr). This is called "Khula" or open
in Arabic. If there is no "good" reason, then the wife has to
follow the Quran:

> Surah al Baqarah 2:229 "Divorce is twice. Then, either keep
> [her] in an acceptable manner or release [her] with good
> treatment. And it is not lawful for you to take anything of what
> you have given them unless both fear that they will not be able
> to keep [within] the limits of Allah. But if you fear that they will
> not keep [within] the limits of Allah, then there is no blame upon
> either of them concerning that by which she ransoms herself.
> These are the limits of Allah, so do not transgress them. And
> whoever transgresses the limits of Allah - it is those who are
> the wrongdoers."

This is a literal ransom the wife pays her husband for her own
freedom. She has to buy herself back. This is another reason
women choose to stay in marriages. They cannot afford the court
costs, the testimony gathering of other women to help her case,
the costs of paying her ransom. There is not even hope of
Paradise for a woman who asks her husband for a divorce when it
is absolutely deemed unnecessary. The Hadith states:

> "Narrated Thawban: The Prophet ﷺ said: If any woman asks
> her husband for divorce without some strong reason, the odor
> (fragrance) of Paradise will be forbidden to her.[60]"

---

[60] Sunan Abu Dawood Vol. 3, Book of Divorce (Kitab Al-Talaq) 13, Hadith
2218

Here is the predicament again as to who determines if it is a "strong reason?"

It is the male rulers which include the Imams, clerics, influential leaders, head of the household, father, brother, or husband who make the decisions in a Muslim community. Women might be able to ask for a divorce - it doesn't mean it will be quickly granted as it would to a man who chooses to divorce for any reason. Divorce affects a woman in a much different way than it does men in a Muslim society. For one, she bears a burden of the shame that she must have been the one to do something wrong. Another reason is because a woman is at home, bearing and rearing children, it is the man who holds the financial accounts and a way to gain income. She will only have the dowry money (if that is still available). Third, many of the influential people in the community are men and it is easy to gather them together to show that if she divorces the man, she will also divorce the community and have no external support. This sets an example to the rest of the women in the community and serves as a warning to not misbehave.

In an article posted on the NPR website titled "Some Muslims in the US Quietly Engage in Polygamy,"[61] there is a story about a woman who was treated as a pariah when her husband divorced her. She was not at fault, yet she was the one who was being

---

[61] Hagerty, B. May 27, 2008. Some Muslims in the U.S. Quietly Engage in Polygamy. https://www.npr.org/templates/story/story.php?storyId=90857818

chastised by the community. Why then are Muslims, even cultural ones, so quick to come to the defense of Islam and say that they are the ones who not only support women's rights, but **protect** them?

The second piece of confusion about divorce comes from the Hadith. The Hadith are traditions of the prophet that were used to explain confusing passages in the Quran. When I was a Muslim, I knew about the Hadith, but there was no access to it. The internet has brought the Hadith to everyone, but even now my friends and other well-meaning Muslims shrug it off - they have the Quran and that's all they need. Since some of them have limited knowledge of the contents, they get traditions and Quran verses mixed up. There are several good websites maintained by Muslims where anyone can find more information on what traditions exist about divorce and women. One just needs to spend time doing research on the web.

Muslim women in the East have privileges, but they have many challenges others do not face that arise from living in countries that utilize Sharia law in their court systems. They do not have the access to freedoms that others in the West enjoy. There are issues and concerns in the Muslim communities around the world that progressive, educated Muslim women are actively striving to address positive change through law, politics and education. While progress has been made over the last few decades, overall, these advances seem to get lost in the male dominated cultures of the Muslim nations. An additional problem occurs when Western ideals get superimposed upon ancient

Islamic systems. Those who desire help from the West find

themselves in the minority for there is a prevailing sense by the

Ummah that they are trying to emulate (what the Muslims believe

to be) a culture of loose morals. Female Muslim reformers not

only have the obstacle of the culture, but also limitations of the

religion, culture, society, roles and duties assigned solely to

women.

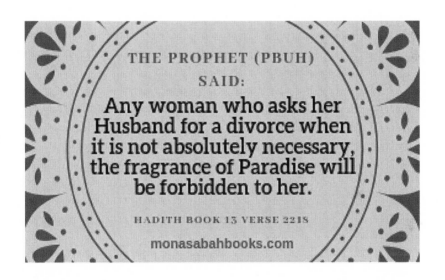

THE PROPHET (PBUH)
SAID:
Any woman who asks her
Husband for a divorce when
it is not absolutely necessary,
the fragrance of Paradise will
be forbidden to her.

HADITH BOOK 13 VERSE 2218

monasabahbooks.com

# Chapter 5

# Muslim Women in the West (USA)

When I share my testimony about what it was like to immigrate to the United States, go to school, then college and graduate school as a Muslim woman, there are many who are surprised to hear about challenges I faced growing up in the United States. Many foreigners see America as a country of freedom, and rightly so, as it provided my parents the opportunity to pursue the American Dream. The United States gave us many freedoms we would not have normally had in Muslim countries as well. As a family, we prospered in areas of finance, education, career, opportunities and society. I try to carefully point out that my experiences as a middle-class Muslim woman should not be applied to all Muslim women, as social standing matters in any society. It is not equitable or fair to paint all Muslim women with a broad brush. Having educated parents meant that we were allowed to pursue not only basic education, but also go to graduate school. We were given rights that other Muslim women don't necessarily have – even in the United States. My parents were progressive thinkers, modern and cultural Muslims. They were not extremist in their views of Islam and have never been - even when they lived in the Middle East.

My family is not the only one who feels this way about Islam in the United States. In a recent (2017) large study done by the PEW Forum Research[62] found that 58% of Muslims in the United States were either immigrants (like me) or children from immigrant (18%) parents. This means that most came to the United States over the last few decades, but it is interesting to note that 26% of immigrants came here after 2000 - after the attacks of 9/11. Integration and assimilation were issues for us. As the young generation, we wanted our freedoms and to enjoy what the country brought us. My parents also wanted freedoms for us, but they wanted that freedom to be tempered by Muslim standards. There is a definite duality that exists. It results in a struggle within families and also an internal struggle for the Muslim living in any Western society.

From the same study (PEW Research 2017), there are interesting statistics of who makes up most of the Muslim population here.

> "Among U.S. Muslim adults who were born abroad, more come from South Asia (35%) than any other region. An additional

---

[62] http://www.pewforum.org/2017/07/26/identity-assimilation-and-community/

23% were born in other parts of the Asia-Pacific region (such as Iran, Indonesia, etc.); 25% come from the Middle East-North Africa region, 9% come from sub-Saharan Africa, 4% were born in Europe and 4% come from elsewhere in the Americas. No single country accounts for more than 15% of adult Muslim immigrants to the United States (15% are from Pakistan). The countries with the next-highest totals are Iran (11% of Muslim immigrants), India (7%), Afghanistan (6%), Bangladesh (6%), Iraq (5%), Kuwait (3%), Syria (3%) and Egypt (3%)."

In terms of diversity, it is more difficult to place all Muslims into one big bucket. There is not a majority in terms of ethnicity. However, people are taken aback when I tell them that those from the Middle East (Arab, Persian, Iraq, Iran, Turkey, etc.) and North Africa are classified as Caucasian or White. The Pew study found that about one-third of Muslims are Asian (28%), including those from South Asia, Pakistan, India and Island countries and one-fifth are black (20%). It is fairly uncommon to see Muslims of Hispanic descent unless they come from Spain and even less to find them self-identify as a "mixed race." Of interest might be the section on how the United States public views Muslims over the last decade as it relates to a change in views on the media and violence.

Over the years, Muslim women in America seem to report a greater dissatisfaction with the media coverage of Muslims. For many, the disconnect was due to their conspicuous dress as it physically set them apart from others and thus, they felt like they were unfairly targeted with negative publicity. Muslim men tend to dress similarly to other American men in jeans, tank tops, shorts, etc. In the brutal heat of the summer months, it is not unusual to see a Muslim man wearing American clothing such as a tank top with shorts and flip flop sandals, while his wife is covered from head to toe in a burqa. I have seen this time and time again in my own community.

There seems to be a shift, however in the Muslim society as the next generation seeks to set their own standards for identity that sets them apart from their parents. My family waned to assimilate into the American culture as quickly as we could. This was an incredibly challenging time for us as we tried to figure out the nuances of American culture. For my mother, wearing a veil was most definitely looked upon as a symbol of oppression as she went to medical school in the 60's in Pakistan - a third world Muslim country. She faced true discrimination as a woman trying to go to graduate school and as she sought work as a professional. She was a rarity among hundreds of men in medical school and was many times, treated with disdain and utter disgust by both the male students and faculty. I grew up believing that the veil was a sign of all that was wrong with Islam and was taught that it was a man-made (again, not stated in the Quran to be covered as in a full burqa) restriction on Muslim women.

This is the only way I can explain it: I think that as the first-generation immigrants try to assimilate, the next generation tries to differentiate. Diversity is a popular notion with today's generation and there is a desire to openly display one's ethnic identity, especially through dress. The media's spotlight has placed the veil center stage, especially in capturing America's attention and imagination. As mentioned in the earlier chapter, a majority of women who report regularly wearing hijab here in the United States said that they wore it in order to secure their identity as a Muslim. In addition, women I have met who wear a hijab have told me that they want to show a visible identity apart from others, including those in their own community (Ummah) who were cultural Muslims. They want to show and wear their religion on the outside and they wanted it to be a clear message that they sent out to the public to prove the sincerity and authenticity of their faith.

After the media coverage of the Taliban in the 2001 war in Afghanistan, the images of truly oppressed women wearing burqas filled the American televisions. I believe this established the notion of the veil as male oppression in Islam for many here in the West. Years later, after books and articles have been written about why women in the West exercise their freedom and choose to cover, there are those who assume that a woman wearing any type of Muslim head covering as being dominated by a male in her family. In the United States, that is just not the case.

In a culture that stands for equality and encourages women being able to compete, look, act and dress like men, the idea of being separated based on dress can chafe others. We are free here to wear jeans, pants, and traditional clothes that men once wore. Women's fight for equality began in the 19th century and continues today. American women, immigrants from Muslim countries and other women don't understand the desire to veil. Events like the one in February 2018, where 29 women in Tehran, Iran were arrested for taking off their hijab to protest against not having civil liberties confuse the American public – is the veil a sign of liberty and freedom of choice or is it oppression? Being raised by a progressive, educated woman, I happen believe that it is a step backwards into time. I have Persian friends here in the States who find the veil disgusting. A highly educated friend of mine was arrested and thrown in jail in Iran for months for speaking out against the veil and for women's rights. She has since sought refuge in the United States and is truly thankful to be here.

The veil is a physical barrier to communication and societal interaction. Not being able to see one's face is not only a physical barrier but can also present a social obstacle and a psychological barrier in terms of fear. The veil also limits what the woman can see out and what other women can see in (such as eye contact). I have a three-layer niqab that I sometimes bring when I teach my course on Islam to promote Christian understanding. When all layers are placed, one can barely see the world around them.

There are Muslim countries that call for little girls wearing a full veil in schools. In America, there is another view that Muslim women are espousing. They are saying that if you take away wearing of religious symbols and ban the veil, you are taking away freedom to dress as they want. They also state that the hijab gives them a modicum of privacy and prevents them from being seen as merely sexual objects, which they claim the West promotes for women. Another phenomenon is when immigrants from Muslim countries have confessed that they never wore the hijab until they came to the United States! Strangely enough, in the Muslim community around the United States, Muslim women who do not veil are being criticized by other Muslims for not sharing in identity with them. I experienced the same when I showed up to a gathering of Muslims in college without a head covering. I was told that I was not being a good Muslim girl. All the while, Muslim women who choose to wear a veil are being looked on with criticism from the American community for not conforming.

It's fascinating to me how some American women are jumping on the veiling bandwagon. There was a well-publicized case from Wheaton College where a Christian professor wore a veil to encourage female solidarity and show that Muslims and Christians worship the same God[63]. While other American women gathered together and put on a hijab to celebrate Muslim women's choice to live modestly and be free to wear a hijab on "World Hijab Day."[64] In February 2018, Macy's Department stores launched a new fashion line, complete with a hijab that is being met with criticisms from Muslims and non-Muslims

---

[63] http://www.chicagotribune.com/news/local/breaking/ct-wheaton-college-professor-firing-reversal-20160206-story.html
[64] http://www.bbc.com/news/av/world-us-canada-38836649/non-muslim-americans-wear-hijab-in-solidarity-for-world-hijab-day

alike.[65] In 2017, Nike launched the Pro Hijab for female athletes.[66] The product was hailed by Muslims, while chastised by others who said it was a ploy to make money from female oppression. The interesting thing is that the final comment made by a female Muslim athlete in an article by the BBC said:

> "I am looking forward for the day where the media stops focusing on such issues and focuses on the person's talent, willpower and human spirit instead of their religious beliefs tied to their opportunity in sports. Sports can't tell whether you're Muslim, Jew, Christian, Aram, African-American, Atheist or one's sexual orientation. It knows talent, whether you can perform or not. This is what makes sports beautiful.[67]"

The quote seems to be placing the blame on the media for focusing on an article of clothing as an issue. Isn't that the whole point of the discussion? Isn't covering up one's head in that fashion proclaiming to the world that you are a Muslim who is playing sports? There are no other religions that mandate such a clothing article for only a part of their population. As a counterpoint, I have seen comparisons made by many between Catholic nuns and Muslims. It's not a legitimate comparison, as the nuns choose to go to a convent. For the Roman Catholics, the

---

[65]Scot, K. (February 20, 2018) Macy's Decisions to Sell Hijabs Sparks Debate Among Muslim Women. https://www.cnn.com/2018/02/17/middleeast/macys-hijab-debate/index.html
[66]The Nike Pro Hijab Goes Global. Dec. 01, 2017 https://news.nike.com/news/nike-pro-hijab
[67] Dawling, E. (January 10, 2018). The sports hijab dividing opinions. Retrieved online. http://www.bbc.com/culture/story/20180110-the-sports-hijab-dividing-opinions

veil signifies something entirely different. No other religion has this stipulation that are placed upon a woman and hinders them.

For an American Muslim, wearing the veil is a prominent statement to defy mainstream culture and not conform to the social standards of this country. Another message being sent out by the veil and the community is that Muslim women are more virtuous than American women. They are taking a stand against immorality and sexual practices of the West. As a Christian woman who believes in modesty, the assumption is incorrect – Muslims believe that everyone who is an American is automatically a Christian. There is a movement taking place in the West that is trying to indoctrinate American society with Muslim traditions and practices on purpose to create a new American norm, including covering the head as a show of consensus and an esprit de corps.

The reasons for Muslim women veiling by choice in America may still remain a mystery as women try to figure out their identities - both as Americans and Muslims. There is a fundamental doctrine of works in Islam and a sense of being a more pious Muslim when wearing a veil. There are others who wear it for identity and still others who wear it because their father or husband are telling them to cover. Whatever the case, it is important to set some of those assumptions aside and simply engage in a conversation with a Muslim woman. One should try to embark on a genuine friendship and find out more about her life, goals, and culture. A hijab should not get in the way or become an obstacle in trying to make a connection, woman to woman. I believe that when one has a desire to truly connect with another as a human is when barriers are broken. Treating one another with respect is a non-negotiable... in any society.

# Chapter 6

# Women in Islam -
# Muhammad's Teachings

The attacks of September 11, 2001 shook up the entire United
States and as a Muslim, I was also moved. I was moved to
sympathy and horror at what happened to my fellow Americans
and I was moved to action in trying to find out what the Quran
actually said about the actions of the terrorists. Of course, I knew
that the media portrayal was a blatant lie—I had never been
taught anything that even resembled closely to what the terrorists
had done. However, all I knew was from tradition and what my
parents had taught me. My uncles, aunts and neighbors, along
with other Muslims in my Ummah were kind-hearted, educated,
professionals, pillars of society and lived relatively quiet lives.
Due to my background in Human Resources and years of

teaching an undergraduate course on Cultural Diversity, I had access to several organizations who hired me to come and speak about Islam and what it was like to live as a Muslim woman in the United States. In order to speak with more authority about Islam, I decided to actually start to live a life of a more pious, practicing Muslim. Granted, I was married to an American man, which put a big dent in the Muslim community's acceptance and their perception of me as being less than "pious," but nevertheless, I was determined to embark on a newer, better, serious Muslim version of myself. I wanted to do works such as start reading the Quran to find out what it truly said about Jihad, to start praying five times a day and to earn favor with good deeds for Judgment Day.

I began a three-and-a-half-year journey into reading the Quran with an English translation. Within a few months, I read a chapter called Surah an Nisa or "The Women." This chapter is written mainly for men and contains instructions on how to marry, inheritance, divorce, children and guidelines on female slaves. Even as I read the Surah, I justified the reading as something I wasn't understanding or misinterpreting from Arabic to English. However, the most disturbing part of reading this chapter was that someone close to me was in the painful process of getting a divorce from her Muslim husband. He did not treat her with respect or kindness, and she was truly an American who was used to having certain freedoms that her Muslim parents allowed.

**Physical Abuse**

The Quran verse 4:34[68] allows for beating a wife even if the husband fears or suspects disobedience, just as it allows for multiple marriages and dominion of the male because it is Allah's will (emphasis mine).

> "Men are in charge of women by [right of] what Allah has given one over the other and what they spend [for maintenance] from their wealth. So righteous women are devoutly obedient, guarding in [the husband's] absence what Allah would have them guard. **But those [wives] from whom you fear arrogance - [first] advise them; [then if they persist], forsake them in bed; and [finally], strike them.** But if they obey you [once more], seek no means against them. Indeed, Allah is ever Exalted and Grand."

Many Muslims argue that the translation falls short on the verse that allows for beating one's wife. Six out of ten translations say "beat (strike) them," while two others say, "scourge them" which means "to whip." Today, there are articles being written that address domestic violence and abuse for Muslim women. In the United States, there were about as many domestic violence reports for Muslims as well as non-Muslims.[69] While the statistics show a similarity on the surface, the difference is that many times, the community does not want to report violence cases due to the honor/shame mindset. They believe that reporting on their family is the same as betraying their religion.

---

[68] http://corpus.quran.com/translation.jsp?chapter=4&verse=34
[69] American Muslim Women and Domestic Violence. August 2, 2017. https://www.domesticshelters.org/articles/race-gender-religion-immigration/american-muslim-women-and-domestic-violence

No matter how it was interpreted, the meaning was clear to me. Since this was the first time, I had ever read anything like this, I couldn't believe it was true. It went contrary to the way I was raised with an affectionate and caring father. I began to question what I was reading, and this questioning was a sign of rebellion! A Muslim person has to believe one hundred percent of what the Quran states because we were taught that it's an authentic document that has never been altered. Even if you question something or say that maybe you are not sure you believe it, you are no longer a Muslim at that point (for reference, see Quran 5:101-102). Unless you believe that all of the Quran is divine revelation from Allah, you cannot be a Muslim.

The freedom that Christians have to openly debate, question, and disagree about things in the Bible are taken for granted by many. Not all, but the average Muslim person is absolutely terrified of entering into a questioning phase when it relates to the Quran. Many elders (parents, Imams, or scholars) consider it to be blasphemy if you question them or the Quran. The culture also dictates a certain respect and submission to authority, so not only is it a religious issue, but also a cultural faux pas to question. It is because of a well-known Hadith[70] of Muhammad that says he hated when too many questions were asked (emphasis mine):

Volume 2, Book 24, Number 555:
 Narrated Ash-sha'bi:
"The clerk of Al-Mughira bin Shu'ba narrated, "Muawiya wrote to Al-

---

[70] http://quotingislam.blogspot.com/2011/06/muhammad-says-allah-hates-when-you-ask.html

Mughira bin Shu'ba: Write to me something which you have heard
from the Prophet (p.b.u.h)." So Al-Mughira wrote: I heard the
Prophet saying, "Allah has hated for you three things:
1. Vain talks, (useless talk) that you talk too much or about others.
2. Wasting of wealth (by extravagance)
3. **And asking too many questions** (in disputed religious
matters) or asking others for something (except in great need)."[71]

Even when I asked my progressive friend's mother questions
about the abuse from her daughter's husband, I could hear anger
in her voice when she asked me why I was questioning the
Quran. I told her I was only questioning why God would allow
half of his creation to be treated in this manner.

**Are Women Truly Worth Half of a Man?**

The evidence should speak for itself. Therefore, I have
included verses here from the Quran in full so that there is no
cherry-picking or taking a verse out of context, for this is a hotly
debated issue among Muslim women who want to say that there
is a misrepresentation of the Quran.

Surah Baqarah 2:282
"O you who have believed, when you contract a debt for a
specified term, write it down. And let a scribe write [it] between
you in justice. Let no scribe refuse to write as Allah has taught
him. So let him write and let the one who has the obligation
dictate. And let him fear Allah, his Lord, and not leave anything
out of it. But if the one who has the obligation is of limited
understanding or weak or unable to dictate himself, then let his
guardian dictate in justice. And bring to witness two witnesses
from among your men. And if there are not two men [available],
**then a man and two women from those whom you accept
as witnesses - so that if one of the women errs, then the**

[71] [71] Sahih al-Bukhari, Vol. 2, Book of Tax (Zakat), Hadith 555 Retrieved
online https://muflihun.com/bukhari/24/555

**other can remind her.** And let not the witnesses refuse when they are called upon. And do not be [too] weary to write it, whether it is small or large, for its [specified] term. That is more just in the sight of Allah and stronger as evidence and more likely to prevent doubt between you, except when it is an immediate transaction which you conduct among yourselves. For [then] there is no blame upon you if you do not write it. And take witnesses when you conclude a contract. Let no scribe be harmed or any witness. For if you do so, indeed, it is [grave] disobedience in you. And fear Allah. And Allah teaches you. And Allah is Knowing of all things."

Surah an Nisa 4:11

"Allah instructs you concerning your children: **for the male, what is equal to the share of two females.** But if there are [only] daughters, two or more, for them is two thirds of one's estate. And if there is only one, **for her is half.** And for one's parents, to each one of them is a sixth of his estate if he left children. But if he had no children and the parents [alone] inherit from him, then for his mother is one third. And if he had brothers [or sisters], for his mother is a sixth, after any bequest he [may have] made or debt. Your parents or your children - you know not which of them are nearest to you in benefit. [These shares are] an obligation [imposed] by Allah. Indeed, Allah is ever Knowing and Wise."

One cannot squelch the factual evidence **that a woman is worth half in Islam**. As mentioned previously in Chapter Two of this book, the female infant gets half of what is given for a male. The woman's testimony in court is worth half, as is a woman's intelligence. There are articles on Sharia law that also state that blood money ("diyah" in Arabic) paid out in case of murder or accidental death is not eye for an eye and tooth for a tooth as stated in the Quran 5:45. Diyah is not the same for Muslim women and men in Muslim legal systems, "because a woman's

life and diyah compensation sentence being half as that of a
Muslim man's life."[72] This is also stated in Hadith:

> "Yahya related to me from Malik that Ibn Shihab and also Urwa
> ibn az-Zubayr said the same as Said ibn al-Musayyab said
> about a woman. Her blood-money from a man is the same up
> to a third of the blood-money of a man. If what she is owed
> exceeds a third of the blood-money of the man, she is given up
> to half of the blood-money of a man."[73]

When researching this law, I came across several Muslim
websites that tried to defend this practice (still being upheld in
Sharia courts) by explaining that a man needs to have more
money than women, who are provided for by their husbands and
fathers. Thus, a woman's life can be paid with a less amount –
even though she is a human being.

The Quran also gives guidance on what to do when the
husband wants to exchange a wife - which apparently a man can
do as long as they do not take back any gifts they have given her
because *that* would be an injustice and not in accordance to the
Quran (not divorcing her, abandoning her or replacing her):

> Surah an Nisa 4:20 "But if you want to replace one wife with
> another and you have given one of them a great amount [in gifts],
> do not take [back] from it anything. Would you take it in injustice
> and manifest sin?"

---

[72] Arsani W. An Unjust Doctrine of Civil Arbitration: Sharia Courts in Canada
and England, Stanford Journal of International Relations, Spring 2010, 11(2),
pp. 40-47
[73] Translation of Malik's Muwatta, Book 43, Number 43.6.4b

As a Muslim woman, I knew that other women did not have it as easy as I did. My father was considerate to his daughters because not only did he allow us freedoms, but also spoiled us rotten. He was doting, loving and caring. From time to time, we would hear stories of Muslim men who had abused women in their family, but this was not the norm for us. My mother would immediately dismiss those types of stories as abnormalities present in other families and not as anything that might be approved behavior. As for marriage, all my family had arranged marriages and my view growing up was that I had to accept it. I was told that it was not an outdated custom, but it was something that strengthened the family and upheld our tradition.

The first time I ever read the Quran, I had to slowly make my way through the unconventional chapters, trying to piece together what Allah had intended to be my purpose as a Muslim woman. Since the Quran is written mainly with men in mind as the audience, it has little to say about any role a woman may have in furthering Allah's agenda. That role seems to be reserved for men only, with women's role revolving around pleasing their husband and dealing with childbirth - especially the Surah on women.

### Aisha & Charge of Adultery

Adultery is a serious offense in many cultures. In Islam, this can get tricky since the man is allowed to have multiple wives and also slaves that his "right-hand possesses" (Surah an Nisa 4:24 -meaning captured slaves from war). When Muhammad's

wife Hafsa caught him in bed with his slave girl (who was a gift -
not a spoil of war) on the night it was her turn and she was
supposed to be with him. It is reported that she got angry and
caused a commotion by telling his favorite wife, Aisha. As the
rules stood at that time, if there were two women who were
witnesses to adultery, then charges could be brought forth.

Shortly after, Allah sent a revelation in the Quran Surah At
Tahrim 66:1-5:

> "O Prophet, why do you prohibit [yourself from] what Allah has
> made lawful for you, seeking the approval of your wives? And
> Allah is Forgiving and Merciful. Allah has already ordained for
> you [Muslims] the dissolution of your oaths. And Allah is your
> protector, and He is the Knowing, the Wise. And [remember]
> when the Prophet confided to one of his wives a statement;
> and when she informed [another] of it and Allah showed it to
> him, he made known part of it and ignored a part. And when he
> informed her about it, she said, "Who told you this?" He said, "I
> was informed by the Knowing, the Acquainted." If you two
> [wives] repent to Allah, [it is best], for your hearts have
> deviated. But if you cooperate against him - then indeed Allah
> is his protector, and Gabriel and the righteous of the believers
> and the angels, moreover, are [his] assistants. Perhaps his
> Lord, if he divorced you [all], would substitute for him wives
> better than you - submitting [to Allah], believing, devoutly
> obedient, repentant, worshipping, and traveling - [ones]
> previously married and virgins."

In this set of verses from the Quran, Muhammad was allowed to
have his oaths and promises be excused by Allah. So basically,
the revelation allowed Muhammad to do whatever he wanted
without penalty and if the wives didn't like it, they would be
substituted with better ones by Allah. He did not need the
approval of his wives and instead, they needed to repent.

**Story of the Lost Necklace**

In Hadith 842,[74] there is an interesting story in which Aisha, Muhammad's favorite wife is accused of adultery due to a lost necklace. Because of the rumors, fights and jealousy between the wives, he would draw lots to see who he would take on a journey with him. Aisha was chosen, and she traveled in a veiled Howda (litter) on a camel. During a break in the journey, she went to answer the call of nature and returned to the camp. When she realized her necklace had fallen off, she returned to look for it. The caravan started off again, including the men lifting the Howda back onto the camel. Aisha said that she was small and light, so they must not have felt any difference in weight.

Upon finding her lost necklace, she ran back to the camp and saw that everyone had packed up and left. She wrapped herself in her cloak, laid down and fell asleep waiting for them to return. A man named Safwan bin Muattal was at the end of the group and reached the place where the rest had stopped earlier. He saw Aisha and put her on his camel to return her back to the group. A man from Muhammad's army named Abdullah bin Ubai bin Salul accused Aisha of adultery and staying behind on purpose to converse with the young man. For months the rumors went on and Aisha finally heard about it from her own mother. She also found out that two tribes (Aus and Khazraj) were getting ready to

[74] http://aHadith.co.uk/Hadithbynarrator.php?n=Urwa+bin+Al-Musayyab%2C+Alqama+bin+Waqqas+and+Ubaidullah+bin+Abdullah&bid=1&let=Q

fight over who was at fault for the rumors and adultery (Sa'd, his companion asked "O Messenger of Allah! Allow me to chop their heads off! Vol. 5, Book 44. Hadith 3180), indeed the penalty for Aisha would also be death. Finally, after a month of the bickering and rumors Muhammad told Aisha that Allah would reveal her innocence or her sin. Shortly after, Muhammad received a positive revelation that exonerated her:

Surah 24:4-8:
"And those who accuse chaste women and then do not produce four witnesses - lash them with eighty lashes and do not accept from them testimony ever after. And those are the defiantly disobedient, Except for those who repent thereafter and reform, for indeed, Allah is Forgiving and Merciful. And those who accuse their wives [of adultery] and have no witnesses except themselves - then the witness of one of them [shall be] four testimonies [swearing] by Allah that indeed, he is of the truthful. And the fifth [oath will be] that the curse of Allah be upon him if he should be among the liars. But it will prevent punishment from her if she gives four testimonies [swearing] by Allah that indeed, he is of the liars."

While Aisha's innocence was maintained, and the rumors quelled, this now created a problem for many other women around the world over centuries. The Quranic revelation asked for four witnesses for guilt or for innocence, thus placing an even larger burden on women (who need two witnesses to one male witness). In a transcript of an interview by an Arab television station (Al Majb TV) Dr. Abd al-Aziz Fawazan al-Fawzan, a professor of Islamic law said that **"if a woman gets raped walking in public alone, then she, herself is at fault. She is only seducing men by her presence. She should have stayed at home like a Muslim**

**woman."**[75]The limitations placed on women weigh heavily on
the lack of freedoms found in the Muslim world because there are
a number of verses yet to be covered:

> "Women are your fields: go, then, into your fields whence you
> please." Quran 2:223
> "And [also prohibited to you are all] married women except
> those your right hands possess. [This is] the decree of Allah
> upon you. And lawful to you are [all others] beyond these,
> [provided] that you seek them [in marriage] with [gifts from]
> your property, desiring chastity, not unlawful sexual
> intercourse. So for whatever you enjoy [of marriage] from them,
> give them their due compensation as an obligation. And there
> is no blame upon you for what you mutually agree to beyond
> the obligation. Indeed, Allah is ever Knowing and Wise." Quran
> 4:24.

"Right hand possesses" means slaves or any women captured
as spoils of war. They are to be used as you wish. Today, Muslim
scholars have to do some word play to get these verses to follow
the anti-slavery sentiment, especially in the West. The distasteful
notion of men taking women as slaves still exists, however, with
a booming sex slave market that flourishes in third world
countries. The verses also state that even in marriage, there is a
type of a contractual obligation because a man should "…give
them their due compensation as an obligation." This is the reason
I was taught as a woman that marriage is not about love, it is a
contract. When men are being instructed on these verses that

---

[75] June 2005 - https://www.memri.org/tv/saudi-cleric-dr-abd-al-aziz-al-
fawzan-explains-why-women-should-not-be-allowed-drive/transcript

idealize male superiority, it plays to the male ego and creates further problems for women all around the world.

## What Awaits Women in Paradise?

In contrast to the restrictions placed here on earth for women, the Quran and Hadith give free sexual freedoms to men on earth and in paradise. In fact, the righteous will be in gardens of pleasure (52:17 & 56:12). Paradise is a very physical and sensual place - there will be ample food, rivers of wine (76:5), (alcohol is forbidden on earth to Muslims) along with milk, honey and lots of virgins for men to take as they wish. They will recline in the shade with couches encrusted with gold and precious stones. They will be married to young, fair-skinned maidens [Houris] with large eyes (52:20) and again:

> "And [for them are] fair women with large, [beautiful] eyes, the likenesses of pearls well-protected, As reward for what they used to do." (56:22-24).

There are a few more descriptions of virgins (a big theme for Paradise):

> "Indeed, We have produced the women of Paradise in a [new] creation And made them virgins devoted to their husbands...as companions (56:35-38)."

The Quran goes on to describe their sexual and physical form in detail, such as "rounded." "a full cup (buxom)," and "as a reward from your Lord" (78:33-34). Various Hadith state that the Houris will be eternal virgins, who are always ready, eager and willing to serve a man's every need.

Surah Al-Insan 76:19-22
"There will circulate among them young boys made eternal.
When you see them, you would think them [as beautiful as]
scattered pearls. And when you look there [in Paradise], you
will see pleasure and great dominion. Upon the inhabitants will
be green garments of fine silk and brocade. And they will be
adorned with bracelets of silver, and their Lord will give them a
purifying drink. [And it will be said], "Indeed, this is for you a
reward and your effort has been appreciated."

It is a fair assumption to make that this is a description of a
reward in Paradise given only for men, as women would not
marry maidens in Islam. Also included in these descriptions are
disturbing verses in several Surahs about men being able to pass
around young boys presented especially for them as if they were
pearls (52:24).

While the Quran differs greatly in its hedonistic descriptions
of Paradise and the afterlife than the Bible, it is thought-
provoking that the Quran gives full chapters to several Biblical
prophets: Jonah, Joseph, and Abraham. Moses is mentioned
mainly in the Surah called "The Cow." Other figures from the
Bible also mentioned in the Quran: Adam, Moses, Aaron, Lot,
Solomon, David, Jacob, Isaac, Noah, Job, Ishmael, Elisha, and
interestingly enough, Zacharias and his son, John the Baptist
(Yahya in Arabic).

In contrast, the Bible presents a clear and concise in the
explanation of paradise (heaven). Jesus said that He would go to
prepare a room for believers in His Father's house. In the book of
Revelation 20 and 21, there are detailed descriptions of what

heaven will look like, but it will surely not be a place of physical pleasures.

Instead, it is a place where angels and believers praise the Lord together without stopping, where God Himself wipes every tear and promises that there will be no more sorrows or pain. It is a place of eternal joy because we get to be in the presence of God.

> "The Bible tells us that after death believers' souls or spirits are taken to heaven, because their sins are forgiven by Christ as Savior (John 3:16, 18, 36). For believers, death is to be "away from the body and at home with the Lord" (2 Corinthians 5:6-8; Philippians 1:23). However, passages such as 1 Corinthians 15: 42-44, 1 Corinthians 15:50-54 and 1 Thessalonians 4:13-17 describe believers being resurrected and given glorified bodies."[76]

No men drinking rivers of alcohol, no Houris and sexual debauchery. For any woman, it truly sounds like heaven.

## Eve in Islam

In a discussion of women in Islam, it is significant to address Adam, Eve and the Creation account from the Bible. Christians are surprised and even confused when I share that Eve's name (Arabic: حواء, Ḥawwā') is not mentioned in the Quran, but that she is called Adam's spouse or wife. The entire Genesis account of Creation is entirely missing in Islam. There are scattered verses of the creation of man, but even that is confusing because one must dig through several chapters to find out what happened.

---

[76] Got Questions. What Happens After Death?
https://www.gotquestions.org/what-happens-death.html

The Quran mentions that creation of the earth took place but says that Adam was created in Heaven by soil taken from the earth. Eve's creation is not mentioned in the Quran at all.

In fact, Eve is only mentioned in a few Hadiths as being taken from a rib, borrowing the information from the Judeo-Christian Scriptures (Sahih Bukhari 4:55:548 and same quote in Sahih Muslim). The Quran does not deign to give Eve her own identity but says the following in Surah an Nisa 4:1:

"O mankind fear your Lord, who created you from one soul and created from it its mate and dispersed from both of them many men and women. And fear Allah, through whom you ask one another, and the wombs. Indeed, Allah is ever, over you, an Observer."

Eve was not her own person but was a part of Adam's soul. To add further differences between Islam and Christianity, modern day Muslims insist that Satan (Arabic شيطان Shaytaan or Shaitan) was not the one who tempted Adam and Eve – it was Iblis [Iblees (إبليس)], another created being who was "of the jinn." Surah al Kahf says in verse 18:50

"And [mention] when We said to the angels, "Prostrate to Adam," and they prostrated, except for Iblees. He was of the jinn and departed from the command of his Lord. Then will you take him and his descendants as allies other than Me while they are enemies to you? Wretched it is for the wrongdoers as an exchange."

The Muslim scholars[77] maintain that angels are noble, created from light (nur or noor in Arabic) and that there are mini-

---

[77] Al Munajjid, Shaykh Muhammad. Islam Q & A website. https://islamqa.info/en/answers/8976/is-iblees-a-jinn-or-an-angel

devilish spirits called **jinn** who cause all the troubles of man (jinn are said to be made from fire- nar in Arabic and that is where we get the word **"genie"** in English). Yet in another verse from Surah al Baqarah 2:34, it states:

> "And [mention] when We said to the angels, "Prostrate before Adam"; so, they prostrated, except for Iblees. He refused and was arrogant and became of the disbelievers."

Iblees (or Iblis) was a part of the angels but some Muslims do not believe he could have been an angel, since they are considered different. Others believe that he may have been an entirely other creation. There is more confusion because just two verses later in the same chapter, the Quran says it was Satan in 2:36?

> "But Satan [Shaytan] caused them to slip out of it and removed them from that [condition] in which they had been. And We said, "Go down, [all of you], as enemies to one another, and you will have upon the earth a place of settlement and provision for a time."

The Fall of man is addressed in several places in the Quran but does not contain the Biblical details and does not mean the same as it does in Christianity. In verses 20:120-123, the Quran addresses how they both ate of the forbidden tree ("the tree of eternity and possession"), that Allah forgave Adam, but both were cast out of Paradise. Here again, are many discrepancies between the clear and careful account in Genesis versus the incomplete one in the Quran. According to the Bible, Adam and Eve were in Eden, located in the land of Cush (Genesis 2:10-14) near the Tigris and Euphrates Rivers that are still present today in southwest Asia (Middle East) – here on earth and not in Paradise.

Allah sent both Adam and Eve to the earth as a result of their actions in Surah 2:37 of the Quran "Then Adam received from his Lord [some] words, and He accepted his repentance. Indeed, it is He who is the Accepting of repentance, the Merciful."

Even though Allah forgave them, it seems that Muhammad did not pardon her, for he blamed Eve for wrongdoing in the Hadith "The Prophet said, "Were it not for Bani Israel, meat would not decay and **were it not for Eve, no woman would ever betray her husband."**[78] A similar Hadith in Sahih Muslim[79] states (emphasis mine):

"Abu Huraira (Allah be pleased with him) reported Allah's Messenger ﷺ as saying: Had it not been for Eve, woman would have never acted unfaithfully towards her husband. Hammam b. Munabbih said: These are some of the aHadith which Abu Huraira (Allah be pleased with him) narrated to us from Allah's Messenger ﷺ, and one of these (this one): Allah's Messenger :dias ﷺ Had it not been for Bani Isra'il, food would not have become stale, and meal would not have gone bad; **and had it not been for Eve, a woman would never have acted unfaithfully toward her husband."**

## No Islamic Concept of Original Sin

There is no doctrine of "original sin" or the Fall of Man in Islam, in fact Muslims see this Biblical doctrine as illogical. In the Quran, Adam and Eve were forgiven (Surah 20:121-

[78] Sahih al-Bukhari Book 55 Hadith 611retrieved online https://muflihun.com/bukhari/55/611
[79] Hadith 3471and 3472, Volume 8 retrieved online https://muflihun.com/muslim/8/3471

122), so there was no hell for them. The Oxford Center for
Islamic Studies[80] explains this in a passage on "Repentance":

> "Arabic tawbah [repentance]. A major theme of the Quran
> mentioned over seventy times and with an entire surah (9)
> titled for it. Usually described as turning toward God, asking
> forgiveness, and being forgiven. Islam has no concept of
> original sin, need for atonement, or ecclesiastical confession.
> Repentance and forgiveness are a direct matter between the
> individual and God, requiring no intercession. In cases of sin
> against another person, restitution is required. In cases of sin
> against God, repentance, remorse, and resolution to change
> one's behavior are considered sufficient. Although classical
> scholars emphasized the individual dimension of repentance,
> many revivalists and reformists have tied individual actions to
> larger issues of public morality, ethics, and social reform,
> arguing for reimplementation of the Islamic penal code as
> public expiation for sins. Sufis understand repentance as a
> process of spiritual conversion toward constant awareness of
> God's presence. Muhammad reputedly requested God's
> forgiveness several times daily."

If there was no original sin, there is no need for a Savior. Man
can accomplish this himself by praying and doing good deeds to
credit his heavenly account daily. Surah an Najm 53:38-48 says:

> "That no burdened person (with sins) shall bear the burden (sins)
> of another. And that man can have nothing but what he does (of
> good and bad). And that his deeds will be seen, then he will be
> recompensed with a full and the best [fair] recompense."

Some Muslim women say that Islam gives a better account of
Eve by giving the blame equally to Adam and Eve and that Allah

---

[80] "Repentance." In The Oxford Dictionary of Islam. Ed. John L. Esposito.
Oxford Islamic Studies Online. 19-Jul-2019.
<http://www.oxfordislamicstudies.com/article/opr/t125/e2004>.

forgave them both equally. Again the Quran, Surah Fatir 35:18
states:

> "And no bearer of burdens will bear the burden of another. And
> if a heavily laden soul calls [another] to [carry some of] its load,
> nothing of it will be carried, even if he should be a close
> relative. You can only warn those who fear their Lord unseen
> and have established prayer. And whoever purifies himself only
> purifies himself for [the benefit of] his soul. And to Allah is the
> [final] destination."

Thus, the Quran is explicit in saying that no one can bear the sins
of another – not even Jesus. You are responsible for your own
good works to tip Allah's scales on Judgment Day. There is only
bad news – there is no Good News of the Gospel in Islam.

From childhood, I was taught that our thoughts are not sinful.
It is acting upon them that could be sinful. If you have a bad
thought and you did not act on it, it could count as a good deed
because you were tempted but didn't do it! How wonderful! This
teaching of Islam is in sharp contrast with what Jesus taught
during his ministry:

> "You have heard that it was said, 'You shall not commit
> adultery.' But I say to you that everyone who looks at a woman
> with lustful intent has already committed adultery with her in his
> heart. If your right eye causes you to sin, tear it out and throw it
> away. For it is better that you lose one of your members than
> that your whole body be thrown into hell. And if your right hand
> causes you to sin, cut it off and throw it away. For it is better
> that you lose one of your members than that your whole body
> go into hell (Matthew 5:27-30)."

Jesus was not just interested in works for works' sake. He was interested in the person's heart, mind, soul and strength (Deuteronomy 6:4).

In the New Testament, the apostle Paul made a clear connection between what Adam did in the Garden to what Christ did for us through His death and resurrection

> "Therefore, just as sin came into the world through one man, and death through sin, and so death spread to all men because all sinned— for sin indeed was in the world before the law was given, but sin is not counted where there is no law. Yet death reigned from Adam to Moses, even over those whose sinning was not like the transgression of Adam, who was a type of the one who was to come. (Romans 5:12-14)."

Again in 1 Corinthians 15:22, it is written, "For as in Adam all die, so also in Christ shall all be made alive."

All of us have sinned. *Muhammad sinned.* Muslims would cringe if they heard anyone say this and they believe it would be blasphemous because some Imams teach that prophets do not sin- especially in the things related to Allah. However, Muslims do believe that prophets are humans and can make mistakes. There are several examples of this in the Quran – Adam (Muslims believe he was a prophet) sinned, Noah in Surah Hud 11:47 asked for forgiveness and mercy, and prophet David asked for forgiveness and repented in Surah Sad 38:24. In addition, the Quran states that Muhammad should ask Allah for forgiveness this in Surah 40:55 and 47:19. A strong and verifiable Hadith states

"'A'isha reported: The Holy Prophet ﷺ entered my house when a Jewess was with me and she was saying: Do you know that you would be put to trial in the grave? The Messenger of Allah no) delbmert ﷺhearing this) and said: It is the Jews only who would-be put to trial. 'A'isha said: We passed some nights and then the Messenger of Allah ﷺ said: Do you know that it has been revealed to me:" You would be put to trial in the grave"? 'A'isha said: 1 heard the Messenger of Allah ﷺ seeking refuge from the torment of the grave after this.[81]

Another strong Hadith adds to the fear of the coming torment

"'A'isha, the wife of the Apostle of Allah ﷺ reported: The Apostle of Allah ﷺ used to supplicate in prayer thus: "O Allah! I seek refuge with Thee from the torment of the grave, and I seek refuge with Thee from the trial of the Masih al-Dajjal (Antichrist) and I seek refuge with Thee from the trial of life and death. O Allah! I seek refuge with Thee from sin and debt." She ('A'isha) reported: Someone said to him - (the Holy Prophet): Messenger of Allah! why is it that you so often seek refuge from debt? He said: When a (person) incurs debt, (he is obliged) to tell lies and break promise.[82]"

Where is the line drawn between a "sin" or a "mistake?" Were the abrogations in the Quran a mistake? If Muhammad was without sin, why did he fear judgment from Allah and torment of hell? Why did he pray to Allah and asking for refuge? Would he not have the confidence of being the "seal of prophets" that he had no sin or no debt to be repaid to Allah?

---

[81] Sahih Muslim, Vol. 2, Book of Prayers, Hadith 1212. Retrieved online https://muflihun.com/muslim/4/1212
[82] Sahih Muslim, Vol. 2, Book of Prayers, Hadith 1218 Retrieved online https://muflihun.com/muslim/4

**Mary in the Quran**

It's such a critical point that it bears to be repeated: there is only one woman who was given the honor of being named in the entire Quran. Not even the prophet Muhammad's favored wife was named -- it is Maryam, or Mary, Jesus Christ's mother. Maryam's chapter is devoted to Isa Masih (pronounced "Eesaw Mahseeh" the Quran's name for Jesus Messiah. He is also called "Isa Ibn Maryam" or Jesus son of Mary) and covers the entire Surah 19.  Growing up as a child in various Muslim countries, I had heard about Prophet Isa Masih, however this was my first time to read anything about the exceptional life of Jesus.

While Muslims are not encouraged to learn about Jesus, Abraham is mentioned frequently in conversation and daily prayer recitations. Most of my cultural Muslim friends do not know much about the other prophets (other than the main ones like Moses- Musa and Jesus – Isa) and when I ask about them, they say that they would rather spend time learning more about their prophet Muhammad. That being said, they are curious and ask questions about the other prophets. I have been asked about Abraham the most, followed by Noah (Nuh) and then others like Adam (who Muslims consider to be a prophet) and David.

Out of women, Mary holds a special standing in Islam. The mother of Christ is hailed by Muslims as one who was pious, came from religiously devoted parents and thus was chosen by Allah to be graced with the miracle of the virgin birth of Christ. The chapter begins with her but does not address Mary. It covers the main points about Isa Masih and his status as a prophet in Islam. I have summarized the important points about Mary in the Quran (Surah Maryam) are summarized in a list for easier reference:

1. She was chosen by Allah to be above all women of the world (3:42)

2. Angels announced to her that she will be the mother of the Messiah, elevated her and his name will be Isa Ibn Maryam (Jesus son of Mary 3:45) and that he was a "pure boy" (19:19)

3. She was chaste and untouched by man (3:47 & 19:20)

Surah At Tahrim 66:12
And [the example of] Mary, the daughter of 'Imran, who guarded her chastity, so We blew into [her garment] through Our angel, and she believed in the words of her Lord and His scriptures and was of the devoutly obedient.

4. She was wrongfully accused of having a child out of wedlock (19:27)

5. Allah called from below her, gave her a stream of water and dates to eat when she gave birth (19:24)

6. Quran states that only two people were born without sin: Mary was pure, as was her son Jesus. **This makes Jesus the only man and prophet who was sinless.**

Sahih Muslim Hadith Book 994 Chapter 30, 5838
"Abu Huraira reported Allah's Messenger as saying: The Satan touches every son of Adam on the day when his mother gives birth to him with the exception of Mary and her son."

There are traditional views of Mary that are incorporated into the Quran and Islamic teaching. She is mistakenly called the sister of Aaron and Moses (Miriam in the Bible) in the Surah. Muslims reading this verse may not catch that Aaron and Moses were alive around 1491 BC, while Christ was born somewhere around 4 BC.[83]

> Surah Maryam 19:28
> "O sister (i.e. the like) of Harun (Aaron) [not the brother of Musa (Moses), but he was another pious man at the time of Maryam (Mary)]! Your father was not a man who used to commit adultery, nor your mother was an unchaste woman."

Another point of interest is that in the Hadith (Ibn Kathir and At Tabarni) Muhammad made a claim that Allah will give Mary (sexually) to him - Mary, the daughter of Imran, as a wife in addition to the other wives he had. This is not a fabricated lie from those who wish to create more issues between Christians and Muslims. Here is a Surah that supports the claim where it states that Allah will give Muhammad additional wives in paradise.

> Surah At Tahrim 66:5
> "Perhaps his Lord, if he divorced you [all], would substitute for him wives better than you - submitting [to Allah], believing, devoutly obedient, repentant, worshipping, and traveling - [ones] previously married and virgins."

[83] Bible Timeline. Retrieved online from website Answers in Genesis. https://answersingenesis.org/bible-timeline/

Online, there seems to be some concern by Muslims who ask whether or not the Hadiths about Muhammad's claim on Isa's mother Maryam are weak. Following is an exchange of a question and answer:[84]

"The Messenger of Allah (peace and blessings of Allah be upon him) entered Khadija in her illness, which she died in. He said to her: I hate what I see of you, Khadija. May God make the good in the heart much better, but I know that God has married me with you in Paradise. The sister of Moses, and Assia the wife of Pharaoh? She said: God did that to you, O Messenger of Allah? He said: Yes, she said: with kindness and kindness. "

The conclusion Muslims can come to is that even though the Hadith given are weak and invalid (per the seven Hadith given on that website), all are still considered to be written Islamic documents -- so at the end of the exchange, the website reports "Each of these Hadiths in its Hadith is considered... God knows."

There are several articles written about this claim on Mary and other treatment of women in Islam even after death in Paradise, including a notable book titled "Women and the Koran" by Anwar Hekmat. There is great difficulty in finding the book, as it is banned in Muslim countries and it is now out of print. A writer for the Middle East Forum online wrote that there are others throughout history, as well as clerics today who attest to

---

[84]Al Munajjid, Shaykh Muhammad. Website Islam Q A. The Hadiths mentioned in the marriage of the Prophet (peace and blessings of Allaah be upon him) in Paradise are from Maryam bint Omran, Asya bint Muzahim, and Kulthum, the sister of Moses https://islamqa.info/ar/answers/111279

this claim of Mary, mother of Christ being one of Muhammad's wives. Ibn Kathir,[85] in his work, as well as cited in Aliah Schleifer's "Mary, The Blessed Virgin of Islam"[86] stated that "The Messenger of God ... said, 'God married me to the daughter of 'Imran and to the wife of Pharaoh and the sister of Moses.' (Tabarani)."[87]

That is to say, not only is Muhammad looked on as someone who surpasses all religions as the "seal of the prophets" in Islam, but he will also upstage others by sexually enjoying another esteemed prophet (Isa's) mother. It is a blasphemy and an affront – not just because of Mary being favored by God, but also because of how that demeans all women as sexual objects who wait around in Paradise for men's carnal pleasure. As a Christian, I thanked the Lord when I read what Jesus Christ said to the Pharisees about heaven in Luke 20:34-35:

> "And Jesus said to them, "The sons of this age marry and are given in marriage, but those who are considered worthy to attain to that age and to the resurrection from the dead neither marry nor are given in marriage..."

As troubling as those verses about Mary are in the Quran, more troubling to me is the stance that many Muslim women take that Islam is a fair religion that treats women equitably,

---

[85] From *al-Mu'jam al-Kabīr*, an early collection of Hadith compiled by Imam Tabarani.

[86] Schleifer, A.. Mary The Blessed Virgin of Islam [Fons Vitae; ISBN: 1887752021; July 1, 1998], p. 64.

[87] From website Answering Islam. Retrieved online https://www.answering-islam.org/Shamoun/mary.htm

reasonably and protects their rights. Women in my family are no exception to this outright defense of Islam. They are vocal about how they are accepted in Islam and are not subjugated in any way. They state the opposite - that Islam allows them freedom of expression as women and they are proud to be from a culture that has made great strides in equality and treats women well. Again, these views come from those who are nominal or cultural Muslims who do not practice Islam or pray, fast, or read the Quran with an understanding. An example is this full review (no editing corrections or deletions) written in 2010 of author Anwar Hekmat's book "Women and the Koran: Status of Women in Islam"[88] online from a Muslim woman[89]

---

REVIEW:
This book is pretty much bashing Islam. As a Muslim Woman, I find myself not close to my faith because of traditional practices. One example is that my brothers can have relations with women, and it is brushed under the rug as "hush hush". Meaning it is accepted. Most Muslim men have slept around numerous times before their marriage to a virgin woman. If I had relations with a man, I could be beaten sevely [sic] and never treated the same again, or kicked out onto the street (in a modern sense).. This is why I want to be celibate all the way to the grave. If am obligated to marry a man I don't know much about, that means I don't have much rights. Let alone sleep with a man who has been around with numerous women before me (a "Zani")..
I don't think this was the book I am looking for. I am not looking for a book that bashes Islam and does child-like name-calling. I am looking for a book that shows what rights Islam provides for

---

[88] Hekmat, A. (1997). "Women and the Koran: Status of Women in Islam." Prometheus Publishing. Amherst, NY.
[89] Customer Review. Nov. 2010 https://www.amazon.com/Women-Koran-Status-Islam/product-reviews/1573921629/ref=cm_cr_arp_d_rvw_fmt?ie=UTF8&reviewerType=all_reviews&sortBy=recent&formatType=current_format

women, and cultural practices that go against Islam. Instead I stumbled upon this book which just makes fun of Islam and is so concentrated about Muhammad. The book title should have Muhammad in it.

Being taught the various stories of Jesus Christ, Abraham and lastly Muhammad, some of the stories in this book don't make sense to me. Islam strictly believes in just 4 wives per man, and the book states that Muhammad had at least 14, 21 at max. And the various bashing that Muhammad "made up" his own religion for his own good.

Well if a man wants to be barbaric and blood-thirsty, he could do that at his own will and not make a religion. There are rulers out there who have killed many people in the past, yet they already followed a religion they didn't make or either don't follow one...

As a Muslim woman...I am more concerned with Islam itself and the Koran. **not Muhammad, Muhammad, Muhammad**. Yes I get he is very important, but I am trying to properly examine the Quran and this book isn't doing it correctly or even politely. I just don't recommend this book. It's very biased and stereotypical. While some believe what this book claims is true (such as Muhammad being a barbaric pedophile), it's not what I am looking for or recommend for others to read. I'd rather be blinded by the "truth" in this book.

Yes women in Islam around the world are treated like objects and given no rights (And even if a Muslim woman has rights, she would still be watched carefully and judged constantly with suspicion.) But this book doesn't focus on women rights...instead it focuses on. Muhammad and stories...

I highly recommend "Qur'an and Woman: Rereading the Sacred Text from a Woman's Perspective" by Amina Wadud. It's what people should be reading than this horribly written book by someone who has a lot of hate.

I wanted to include the entire review because it shows the reasoning of a Muslim mind. It also serves as a good example of what I personally experienced and my thought process as a Muslim woman. I was trying to find out what Islam and Allah had to offer me. I had many questions like "Why was I created?" "What should I do for Allah to repay him for my life/my kids/my house/my job?" but all I concluded after reading the Quran was that it was truly a religion that was based upon *"Muhammad, Muhammad, Muhammad"* as the woman in the book review said.

In trying to present a full view of what Islam presents and what the Quran and Hadith teach, again there are multiple references[90] that will make the point about what Muhammad thought about women (emphasis mine):

> Narrated by al-Bukhari, 3241; Muslim and 2737 Narrated by al-Bukhari, Vol.1, Book 6, 301 and Vol. 3, Book 48, 826[91]
> "It was narrated that Abu Sa'eed al-Khudri (may Allah be pleased with him) said:
>
> "The Messenger of Allah (peace and blessings of Allah be upon him) went out to the musalla (prayer place) on the day of Eid al-Adha or Eid al-Fitr. He passed by the women and said, **'O women! Give charity, for I have seen that you form the majority of the people of Hell.' They asked, 'Why is that, O Messenger of Allah?' He replied, 'You curse frequently and are ungrateful to your husbands. I have not seen anyone more deficient in intelligence and religious commitment than you.** A cautious sensible man could be led astray by some of you.' The women asked, 'O Messenger of Allah, what is deficient in our intelligence and religious commitment?' **He said, 'Is not the testimony of two women equal to the testimony of one man?' They said, 'Yes.' He said, 'This is the deficiency in her intelligence. Is it not true that a woman can neither pray nor fast during her menses?' The women said, 'Yes.' He said, 'This is the deficiency in her religious commitment.'"**

It is difficult to justify or vindicate a religion that teaches as a tradition that women are deficient in their minds and also in their

---

[90] Al Bukhari. Hadith Book of Wedlock, Marriage, Nikaah.
https://sunnah.com/bukhari/67/132
[91] Sahih al-Bukhari, Book 6 of Menstrual Periods, Hadith 301 retrieved online https://muflihun.com/bukhari/6/301 and https://muflihun.com/bukhari/48/826

religious commitments to Allah due to no fault of their own, but the fault lies in the way they were created (to have a menstrual cycle which hinders them naturally or physically from being able to pray or fast) should speak for itself. According to the Hadith above, not only did Muhammad chastise the women who came out to pray on a festival day, but also told the gathered that they were going to Hell "… for I have seen that you form the majority of the people of Hell." When they asked why, the answers given blamed the women for everything from being ungrateful, to tempting men, to them being worth half in testimony, to their intelligence and to their lack of religious commitment due to something natural – bleeding. In the Quran, Surah an Nisa verse 4:43 states:

> "O you who have believed, do not approach prayer while you are intoxicated until you know what you are saying or in a state of janabah, except those passing through [a place of prayer], until you have washed [your whole body]. And if you are ill or on a journey or one of you comes from the place of relieving himself **or you have contacted women and find no water,** then seek clean earth and wipe over your faces and your hands [with it]. Indeed, Allah is ever Pardoning and Forgiving."

Even touching women makes a man unclean. Why? Because women are unclean. To be fair, Islam is not the only religion that says this about women. For the orthodox Jews, touching a woman who was not a relative and touching a bleeding woman made the man unclean and thus, unfit for prayer to God.

When media articles about Muslim clerics who publish pamphlets on how to beat your female slaves are published, it is like adding fuel to the fire. An article in 2014 appeared in the Washington Post about videos from the Islamic State on how to treat the Yazidi women they had kidnapped (upwards of 2,500)[92]. The laws come from several Hadiths on owning female slaves, such as this one:

> "Malik related to me from Nafi that Safiyya bint Abi Ubayd informed him that Umar ibn al-Khattab said, "What is the matter with men who have intercourse with their slave-girls and then leave them to go? No slave-girl comes to me whose master confesses that he has had intercourse with her but that I connect her child to him, whether or not he has practised coitus interruptus or left off from intercourse with her."Yahya said that he heard Malik say, "What is done in our community about an umm walad who commits a crime is that her master is liable for what she has done up to her value. He does not have to surrender her, and he cannot be made to bear more than her value for her crime.[93]"

Or how about this one, among many others?
> Narrated Abu 'Abdur-Rahman As-Sulami:
> "Ali gave a Khutbah, and said: 'O people, establish the penalties upon your slaves, those married from them and those unmarried. A slave girl of the Prophet ☀committed illegal sexual intercourse **so he ordered me to whip her**. I went to her and she was just experiencing her post-natal bleeding, so I feared that if I were to whip her I would kill her – or he said: 'She would die' – 'so I went to the Messenger of Allah I dna ☀ told that to him. So he said: 'You did well.'[94]"

Or in the Hadith Book of Good Manners
> "Narrated 'Abdullah bin Zam'a:

---

[92] Tharoor, I. Dec. 12, 2014
https://www.washingtonpost.com/news/worldviews/wp/2014/12/12/the-islamic-state-issues-guide-on-when-its-okay-to-beat-your-sex-slave/?noredirect=on&utm_term=.e362cf51d31d

[93] Muwatta Imam Malik, Book 36 of Judgements, Hadith 25 Retrieved online
https://muflihun.com/malik/36/25

[94] Jami` at-Tirmidhi, Vol. 3, Book of Legal Punishments, Hadith 1441
Retrieved online https://muflihun.com/tirmidhi/17/1441

The Prophet forbade laughing at a person who passes wind, and said, "How does anyone of you beat his wife as he beats the stallion camel and then he may embrace (sleep with) her?" And Hisham said, "As he beats his slave[95]"

## Another one states simply

"It was narrated that Ash'ath bin Qais said: "I was a guest (at the home) of 'Umar one night, and in the middle of the night he went and hit his wife, and I separated them. When he went to bed he said to me: 'O Ash'ath, learn from me something that I heard from the Messenger of Allah" A man should not be asked why he beats his wife, and do not go to sleep until you have prayed the Witr.'" And I forgot the third thing.[96]"

## On wife beating, he was more lenient for he told the men to stop… but then told them to go ahead again

"Iyas ibn Abdullah ibn Abu Dhubab reported the Messenger of Allah ﷺ as saying:
Do not beat Allah's handmaidens, but when Umar came to the Messenger of Allah ﷺ and said: Women have become emboldened towards their husbands, **he (the Prophet) gave permission to beat them.** Then many women came round the family of the Messenger of Allah ﷺ complaining against their husbands. So the Messenger of Allah ﷺ said: Many women have gone round Muhammad's family complaining against their husbands. They are not the best among you.[97]"

To sum up the Hadith verses, wife beating is allowed as is owning female slaves. The conclusion I came to was that a Muslim woman who is trying to do every good deed she is able to do, and a man who tries to do every good deed he can, would always result in the man receiving a higher reward from Allah

[95] Sahih al-Bukhari, Vol. 8, Book of Good Manners, Hadith 68 Retrieved online https://muflihun.com/bukhari/73/68
[96] Sunan Ibn Majah, Vol. 3, Book of Marriage, Hadith 1986 Retrieved online https://muflihun.com/ibnmajah/9/1986
[97] Sunan Abi Dawood, Vol. 2, Book of Marriage (Kitab Al-Nikah), Hadith 2141 Retrieved online https://muflihun.com/abudawood/12/2141

because he was able to do more religious deeds. There are no physical restrictions placed upon a male. This was the issue I faced, and I had no choice as a Muslim woman. I wept after childbirth because I knew that Allah would not permit me to pray or approach him in any way during this time. I was drowning in a prayer deficit from the daily obligatory five prayers and had no way possible to make them up. What if I died before I could make up my missed prayers?

Why would Allah design the female to do less works and have restrictions put forth upon her that were beyond her control? Why did he predestine women for hell in their physical make up and create another chasm for them to overcome by themselves? *What privilege in Islam is there to for Muslim women to defend?*

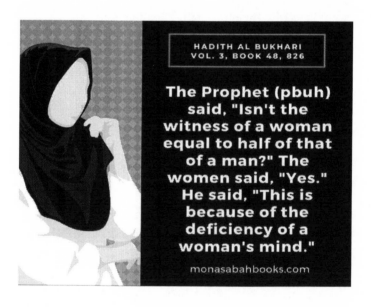

HADITH AL BUKHARI
VOL. 3, BOOK 48, 826

The Prophet (pbuh) said, "Isn't the witness of a woman equal to half of that of a man?" The women said, "Yes." He said, "This is because of the deficiency of a woman's mind."

monasabahbooks.com

# Chapter 7

# Women in the Bible -
# Jesus' Teachings

One of the most startling things for me as a new believer in Christ was the honest portrayal and transparency of the Bible. As a Muslim, I was taught that Abraham was a paragon to uphold, that he was faultless in his faith and that he was perfect (even though the Quran does not call him perfect, that was what most Imams teach in the mosque and thus Muslims believe that about all the prophets). The same was true for David that he was a true leader, someone to be looked up to and was blameless in Allah's sight. It became evident to me quickly that Islam did not teach about prophets in the same way the Bible does. When I read Genesis, I saw that Abraham lied and not just once but several times. In fact, his lie was confronted by a pagan king who called him out and told him to set things straight by the God he

worshipped. When I read about David, I almost fell out of my
seat when I read about David's adultery with Bathsheba and the
way the Lord punished him for it. Neither man was blameless or
perfect.

The same holds true for the apostles in the New Testament.
They are shown with their shortcomings, tempers, doubts, fears,
and disbelief. Through it all, Jesus Christ alone is entirely
blameless and sinless.  Jesus is unique in the Bible and he is
unique in the Quran as well. He stands out as a prophet who does
the most miracles, was pure from birth, and is the only man the
Quran calls sinless (Quran 19:19 *ghulaaman-zakiyya* meaning "a
pure boy" where *zakiyya* means "blameless").

Even Muhammad was told in the Quran to ask for forgiveness
for his sins in Surah al Tawbah verse 9:43 and Surah Gafir 40:55:

"May Allah pardon you, [O Muhammad]; why did you   give
them permission [to remain behind]? [You should    not have]
until it was evident to you who were truthful, and you knew
[who were] the liars."

Surah Gafir 40:55
"So be patient, [O Muhammad]. Indeed, the promise of Allah is
truth. And ask forgiveness for your sin and exalt [Allah] with
praise of your Lord in the evening and the morning."

Yet another verse in Surah Muhammad 47:19 states more clearly

"So know, [O Muhammad], that there is no deity except Allah
and ask forgiveness for your sin and for the believing men and
believing women. And Allah knows of your movement and your
resting place." Hadith stated this even more clearly "Abu
Huraira reported: The Messenger of Allah ﷺ used to say while

prostrating himself: O Lord, forgive me all my sins, small and great, first and last, open and secret."[98]

I couldn't wait to read what the New Testament had to say about Jesus, my Lord and Savior and his interactions with women. I was not sure what to expect, as a brand-new Christian who had lived in the United States for over two decades, I had still not heard much about Jesus. The Gospels (first four books of the New Testament that encapsulate Jesus Christ's ministry on earth) were very interesting. I was not sure why I was reading the same story four times, but I saw that each account had a different element to it. I later found out that they are called the "synoptic" Gospels (Matthew, Mark, and Luke), which means similar point of view ("syn" is Greek for similar and "optic" is Greek for eye, view, or vision).

When Jesus Christ was born in first century Palestine, the world discriminated heavily against women. Most scholars would agree that women were treated as second class citizens and held little, if any rights in society. In their book "Woman in the World of Jesus," Frank and Evelyn Stagg (1979)[99] researched and found that there were a high number of references to women in the Gospels. In all interactions, Jesus sets the standard for treatment for women in a culture that had rules against equality of women - as in Islam, there are rules against men addressing

[98] Sahih Muslim, Vol. 1, Book of Prayers, Hadith 980 Retrieved online https://muflihun.com/muslim/4
[99] Ryan, R. (1979). Woman in the World of Jesus. By Evelyn and Frank Stagg. Philadelphia: The Westminster Press, 1978.

women in public. In reading the New Testament, Jesus does not belittle women or disparage them in any way. He treats women with respect, openly engages them in dialogue and even defends them to the Pharisees (keepers of the Old Testament laws).

### *Mary, Mother of Jesus*

The LORD begins Jesus' time on the earth by bestowing great favor on Mary. She is the first woman mentioned in the Gospel books as the mother of Christ. Her unquestioning faith is still celebrated worldwide as she proclaims the name of God in the Gospel of Luke (1:46-55) a song of praise that is called "Magnificat" (Latin for "magnifies" - the prayer begins with "My soul magnifies the Lord"). She showed great obedience to God when she was visited by an angel who revealed to her that even though she was a virgin, she would bear a child, "The Holy Spirit will come upon you, and the power of the Most High will overshadow you; and for that reason the holy child shall be called the Son of God" (Luke 1:35). She had to endure a possible divorce from Joseph (her betrothed) and did not have rich, luxurious amenities for her baby's delivery, for Luke 2:7 states "And she gave birth to her firstborn son and wrapped him in swaddling cloths and laid him in a manger, because there was no place for them in the inn."

The very first miracle of Jesus' ministry involves His mother Mary and it is presented in the Gospel of John, chapter 2 when Mary tells Jesus at a wedding feast in Cana, that the host has run out of wine. Mary wanted her son to solve this problem for the wedding guests. Jesus responds to her by saying "Woman, what does this have to do with me? My hour has not yet come" (John 2:4). I have heard great debate in women's Bible studies and read articles on how some might perceive this response as Jesus being rude to his mother. In modern English, we may see calling one's mother "woman" as being harsh, offensive or even a bit too casual. In that time and in the language (Aramaic or Hebrew) of Jesus this may have not been the case. Instead, Jesus was simply giving his mother a reminder that she did not dictate the time for miracles – that he did not do them at her command, but at the time that was ordained by God. To further substantiate this, later when his mother wept for him at the foot of the cross and watching her son suffer a cruel punishment, the Bible states, "When Jesus saw his mother and the disciple whom he loved standing nearby, he said to his mother, 'Woman, behold, your son! Then he said to the disciple, "Behold, your mother!" And from that hour the disciple took her to his own home.'" (John 19:26-27). It's interesting that no one doubts the love and tenderness Jesus showed his mother in telling her that his disciple would now be entrusted with her care, yet some choose to argue about the use of the same descriptive word "woman" in the earlier passage.

Mary bore Jesus, took care of him, saw prophecies fulfilled, saw him tortured, crucified, buried, and then was a witness to his resurrection! The Bible tells us that she was favored over all women and she was the mother of the Messiah of God. Her name and status among women is elevated and she is given great honor throughout the world.

It should be noted that "Mary" is a common name that appears again and again in the New Testament. There are several different women named Mary – Mary the mother of Jesus - Matthew 1:16, Mary the sister of Lazarus (also called Mary of Bethany) – John 11:1, Mary the mother of James and Joseph - Matthew 27:56, Mary the wife of Clopas - John 19:25, Mary Magdalene (most likely Mary from the town of Magdala, west of the Sea of Galilee) – Luke 24:10, etc. Jesus not only interacted with His mother in the Gospels but also with these and many other women throughout His ministry on earth.

### *Mary and Martha – Sisters of Lazarus*

Mary and Martha are two sisters whose story is related to us in the Gospel accounts as women who had direct contact and meaningful conversations with Jesus. Their descriptions show just how different they were in their temperament and priorities. The two sisters are contrasted in their personalities in the following verses:

> "So when Martha heard that Jesus was coming, she went and met him, but Mary remained seated in the house." John 11:20
> "So they gave a dinner for him there. Martha served, and Lazarus was one of those reclining with him at table." John 12:2

The scene is set as Jesus entered the village of Bethany and their home in Luke 10:38-42:

> "Now as they went on their way, Jesus entered a village. And a woman named Martha welcomed him into her house. And she had a sister called Mary, who sat at the Lord's feet and listened to his teaching. But Martha was distracted with much serving. And she went up to him and said, 'Lord, do you not care that my sister has left me to serve alone? Tell her then to help me.' But the Lord answered her, 'Martha, Martha, you are anxious and troubled about many things, but one thing is necessary. Mary has chosen the good portion, which will not be taken away from her.'"

Martha welcomed, but Mary stopped what she was doing in order to sit still and listen to Jesus. In Gill's Exposition of the Bible[100], there is a verse in Acts 22:3 where Paul studies "at the feet of Gamaliel" and that passage is explained here:

> "a custom of scholars among the Jews, to sit at the feet of their masters, when instructed by them; see Deuteronomy 33:3 hence that saying of Jose ben Joezer (a); "let thy house be an house of resort for the wise men, and be thou dusting thyself, "with the dust of their feet":" which by one of their commentators (b) is interpreted two ways, either "as if it was said that thou shouldst walk after them; for he that walks raises the dust with his feet, and he that goes after him is filled with the dust which he raises with his feet; or else that thou shouldst sit at their feet upon the ground, for so it was usual, that the master sat upon a bench, and the scholars sat at his feet upon the floor."

While one can see that Martha was using her gift of hospitality and service, it was the calm, contemplative Mary who was lauded by Jesus as the one who had chosen the right thing to

---

[100] http://biblehub.com/commentaries/gill/acts/22.htm

do. We can learn from the sisters that while our service is pleasing to God, it should not be done at the expense of study or missing entirely the word of God. Also it implies that works are not what God wants from us. *Our main work is to be immersed in His presence to gain a relationship that is dependent upon Him for our every need.*

As Jesus spoke to Martha in the passage above, his tone was not one of derision. He says her name twice "Martha, Martha," which in the Old Testament and New Testament indicates a term of deep endearment; God only does this with a handful of prophets - Abraham, Jacob, Moses, Samuel and Saul who becomes Paul. So, in saying her name twice, he bestowed upon her a great honor and show of love in the Bible!

In contrast to Martha's preparation for dinner, Jesus not only allows Mary to remain at his feet but instructed Martha that it was more important to be in His presence to learn than to busy herself with dishes. This would be a complete surprise to all who would be within earshot, for women were never considered worthy of being disciples or students of a Rabbi! They were not allowed to sit and learn in the synagogue. According to both cultural and social standards, Martha was correct - she and her sister should have been engaged in the preparation and serving of the guests, just as she was doing.

But Jesus was not there to cater to culture. He was quintessentially counter-cultural in His behavior. He wanted both of these women to come and sit close to Him, learn from Him, spend time with Him as their teacher. Even today in the Middle East, this is not standard practice. While women attend both regular and religious school, they learn from female teachers when they are older (past puberty). To have a man come to the women to offer to instruct them was not permitted or practiced. It is also customary today in the Middle East that female students can only learn from female teachers at school. Muslims try to counter this claim by saying that both Muhammad's wives Khadijah and Aisha taught Islam. That is true, but women who were scholars and taught men in Islam were far and few in between, with much of the Muslim world today separating out men and women in any type of a social gathering. Even for Biblical times, with the lens of the modern Western world, it is sometimes difficult to see the implications of a grown woman sitting at a man's feet (especially one who was not related to her).

This family was near and dear to Jesus. Later in the Gospel accounts, Mary and Martha's brother Lazarus died and was buried in a tomb while Jesus was away. The two sisters were distraught and were weeping at their great loss when Jesus came to comfort them. Mary again fell to her Lord's feet:

"When the Jews who were with her in the house, consoling her, saw Mary rise quickly and go out, they followed her, supposing that she was going to the tomb to weep there. Now when Mary came to where Jesus was and saw him, she fell at his feet, saying to him, "Lord, if you had been here, my brother would not have died.' When Jesus saw her weeping, and the Jews who had come with her also weeping, he was deeply moved in his spirit and greatly troubled" John 11:31-33.

Later in the passage Jesus restored Martha and performed the

miracle of raising their brother Lazarus from the dead in John

11:25-26 when he revealed who he truly is:

> "Jesus said to her, 'I am the resurrection and the life.  Whoever
> believes in me, though he dies, yet shall he live, and everyone who
> lives and believes in me shall never die. Do you believe this?"

To which she confessed correctly in the next verse (11:27),

"She said to him, 'Yes, Lord; I believe that you are the Christ,

the Son of God, who is coming into the world.'"

Jesus broke down the cultural barriers that existed in

Jerusalem and all over the Middle East. This was not just a

revolutionary statement made for that time and place. In John 12,

the Bible describes a profound passage where the same Mary of

Bethany came into a dinner party where her sister Martha served

the guests while their brother Lazarus was seated near Jesus. She

carried in her hands an alabaster jar of rich perfume called nard.

Nard was precious and dear, considered to be an item of great

luxury for a woman. The Bible account states that the contents of

the jar were 300 denarii (about one year's wages), in addition, we

do not know the cost of the alabaster jar. In front of mixed

company at someone else's home, she broke the jar and poured

out the entire contents on the head of her Lord and Savior, Jesus

Christ. As if that was not shocking enough to the guests, she

unbound her hair (something a Middle Eastern woman would

never do in public, much less in front of a man who was not her husband) and in a most physical, intimate way, wiped the perfume on his feet with her hair. The account in the book of John (12:1-8) states that "The house was filled with the fragrance of the perfume." Not only was this a lavish display of worship, it was a literal fragrant offering to the Lord.

As Judas witnessed this act, instead of seeing the devotion and anointing upon his master for burial that was to come, he only saw money being wasted (John 12:5). The other disciples were also "indignant" at the wasted perfume. What the world deems as wasteful, the Lord accepts as a proper, loving response. In today's terms, Mary "threw away" almost 45,000 dollars (one year's average wage in the United States) worth of perfume on Jesus – what would your friends say if you wrote a check for your full salary and dropped it off at church? I wonder if the complaints would echo the same indignation that was voiced or maybe you might be called a zealot who was going overboard?

She was most likely a single woman, for she was always noted in the accounts with her sister and brother, so she would not have had much of her own income. Some scholars have speculated that since the perfume was in an alabaster jar, it may have been a costly family heirloom. No matter what the background was, Mary showed unreserved reverence for Jesus Christ in her devotion that cast aside the cultural traditions and restrictions placed upon any woman at that time. Jesus accepted this extravagant form of public worship and she is forever listed in the Scriptural accounts as a woman to be praised.

Not only were the sisters Mary and Martha in the immediate group of disciples, but there were other women who joined and appeared throughout the New Testament. Luke 8:1-3 states:

> "Soon afterward he went on through cities and villages, proclaiming and bringing the good news of the kingdom of God. And the twelve were with him, and also some women who had been healed of evil spirits and infirmities: Mary, called Magdalene, from whom seven demons had gone out, and Joanna, the wife of Chuza, Herod's household manager, and Susanna, and many others, who provided for them out of their means."

Here, Jesus allowed women as well as men to join him, travel distances from town to town with him, but women also to help support the ministry. It was surprising to me that the author Luke mentioned women who seemed to be in positions of honor (such as wife of the manager of Herod the King's household) helped to pay as they were able. Later, in the New Testament book of Acts, there was another wealthy woman named Lydia who financially supported the work of the apostle Paul and the early Christian church through her status as a businesswoman who provided purple cloth to royalty.

### The Samaritan Woman at the Well

Samaritans were despised by the Jews for they were not considered to be true believers in the covenant of Abraham. They would not mingle with the people of Samaria and they treated them as people who were unclean because they rejected most of Jewish law. From Jewish history, Samaritans were people of

Ephraim and a part of Manasseh[101] (2 Kings 17:24-28) who intermarried with foreigners and worshipped idols. In John 4:9, it states that the Jews had no dealings with the Samaritans. In the New Testament, Jesus shared the story of the "Good Samaritan" (see Luke 10:25-37) where he gave the outsider (a Samaritan) the description of being "good." He contrasted the Samaritan's act of mercy and servanthood to the Levites and Pharisees, as they disregarded another human being's need for care and sympathy. Even though they were the religious leaders of Israel, Jesus instead elevated a mere Samaritan in the parable.

Once again in His ministry, Jesus went out of his way to have a divine appointment with a woman in Samaria who is drawing water at the hottest part of the day (John 4). The time of day is important because most women tended to draw water in the early morning for cooking and cleaning and then again in the evening for washing. There is a verse in Song of Solomon 1:7, stated that even shepherds rested their flocks during that time of day. Today, villages in the East have a similar routine. I remember staying at my father's village home in Pakistan in the Summer months to see this ritual take place for myself when I was a little girl, not understanding the significance and context it would give me later as I read the story in the Bible. Early in the morning, when the day was just beginning to start, the modest home with its dirt floor would begin to awaken with noise. I would rise up and go

---

[101] Who were the Samaritans? https://www.gotquestions.org/Samaritans.html

outside to the courtyard and the low dirt and stone walls would allow me to see the local women gathered at the well, chattering away about their work for the day with their babies on one hip and a clay water vessel on the other. They would discuss who was visiting, what the children and husbands were doing and what dishes they were set to prepare. The gathering was repeated in the cool of the evening when the sun was getting ready to set, as some of the women returned to fill their jars for the evening prayer ablutions as well as dinner for the family.

In the passage, this particular woman comes to the well with her vessel (usually a clay or skin vessel with a cup or a closure on top) in the afternoon by herself, for there is no one else there to give Jesus a drink. She not only noticed his lack of a cup but also saw that he wanted to engage her in a conversation. It is important to note that this was a Rabbi who initiated a conversation with a solitary, despised Samaritan woman. Not only did he speak to her, but he asked her help to share her cup with him. This would mean that he would be unclean after drinking from a vessel that belonged to a woman and a Samaritan! The absurdity of the situation was not lost on her. Neither was the great social divide between the Jews and the outside world. His words were an invitation to see the gift of God being given to all nations through Christ.

Jesus replied to the woman by saying "...If you knew the gift of God, and who it is that is saying to you, 'Give me a drink,' you would have asked him, and he would have given you living water

(John 4:10)." Jesus referred to himself as the gift of God. She would have possibly recognized that the gift of God for the Jews was the Torah given to Moses. Muslims would not understand this verse either, for their belief is that the gift of Allah is the Quran. However, Jesus showed here that He is the veritable word of the living God and the source of life. It is no coincidence that Jesus is seated at the well of Jacob - an ancient well that was still bringing forth water to a thirsty land. Jesus showed himself to be the culmination of all Old Testament laws and prophets by referring to himself in this way. In his book "Mere Christianity," British author C. S. Lewis said:

> A man who was merely a man and said the sort of things Jesus said would not be a great moral teacher. He would either be a lunatic — on the level with the man who says he is a poached egg — or else he would be the Devil of Hell. You must make your choice. Either this man was, and is, the Son of God, or else a madman or something worse. You can shut him up for a fool, you can spit at him and kill him as a demon, or you can fall at his feet and call him Lord and God but let us not come with any patronizing nonsense about his being a great human teacher. He has not left that open to us. He did not intend to.[102]"

Who else would refer to himself as a gift of God who gives living water? That would not even make sense unless there was an understanding of Scripture of living water (Jeremiah 2:13) and the expectation of a coming Messiah. Just as she failed to grasp

[102] Lewis, C. S. (2001). *Mere Christianity: A revised and amplified edition, with a new introduction, of the three books, Broadcast talks, Christian behaviour, and Beyond personality* (1st HarperCollins ed.). San Francisco: Harper SanFrancisco.

his meaning and just as many who hear this story for the first time don't understand the depth and importance of what Jesus claimed to be – Emmanuel, God with us.

She initiated questions to find out if he was serious about speaking with her and then tried to discern what he said to her (she knew he was a prophet - John 4:19). The interview is most fascinating to me as it culminates with Jesus telling her that he is the Messiah. As the disciples showed up with food they went to get, they were puzzled at why Jesus was engaged in a conversation with a woman. Even they were not sure about what he was doing and why did he want to speak to her? As the conversation progressed, "Jesus said to her, "Go, call your husband, and come here (John 4:16)." In this verse, He gave her three commands: go, call, come back with him. When she replied that she had no husband, we do not know if she was trying to hide the truth that she was now living with another man or if she was trying to evade the question. But Jesus already knew the answer:

> "The woman answered him, "I have no husband." Jesus said to her, "You are right in saying, 'I have no husband'; for you have had five husbands, and the one you now have is not your husband. What you have said is true." The woman said to him, "Sir, I perceive that you are a prophet. (John 4:17-19)."

Jesus then revealed to her that he was the Messiah for whom her people were waiting. She immediately left her water jar and ran to tell the people of her town about this man who knew her scandalous past and that she was presently living with another man.

She didn't dwell upon her honor/shame. She didn't think of herself at all but went unabashedly to share the news of Jesus and asked others to come and see for themselves. One can almost hear the urgency and excitement, mingled with awe in her invitation to others. People took her at face value, for they believed in Christ because of the woman's testimony and the townspeople further showed Jesus hospitality by asking him to stay for a few days. John 4:41-42 says:

> "Many more believed because of his word. They said to the woman,
> 'It is no longer because of what you said that we believe, for we have heard for ourselves, and we know that this is indeed the Savior of the world.'"

What an example for us to see how the Lord showed His mercy to a woman who was an outcast and then entrusted her with a message for the world. In Islam, a prophet or even a holy man (Imam or cleric) would not have approached an unmarried woman in broad daylight. We know, however, that this was no ordinary woman. She was not respectable for she was living in sin with a man in ancient times - none of the women from her town would associate with her, for she went to the well alone. For a male stranger to ask a female to share her personal eating or drinking vessel with him was an intimate suggestion. Only family members could do that and even then, in Muslim families, daughters do not share with fathers as they are elevated in status above the rest of the family. How much higher would a Rabbi be in society? I cannot imagine sharing my water bottle with my dad and especially not an Imam! The thought would have never entered my mind and would have been absolutely controversial and even provocative to others if they found out something like that would have happened. In His discourse, Jesus never became angry with her. He did not chastise her for living with a man to whom she was not married - just that sin alone would have resulted in her being stoned to death. He did not rebuke her or become angry with her... instead, he honored her when gave her a revelation and the ultimate gift of grace on her life. *He gave her the gift of God.*

As Christians, we can learn a lot from this woman. When we go (like the woman did), call out to others to share who Christ is and tell how he has seen into the darkest part of our soul, suddenly there is illumination and that light breaks free to shine on to those who listen. Because of the freedom and joy that comes from understanding who Jesus Christ is and what He has done on our behalf, we should be compelled to share the good news of the Gospel message - that Jesus Christ is who he said he is, and that he has come to give us his living water, so we will never be thirsty again. "The water that I will give him will become in him a spring of water welling up to eternal life -John 4:14." The beauty of this message is that it goes out to the Jews and the Gentiles alike and it goes out to both men and women alike.

## The Bleeding Woman

In three of the four Gospels, Luke (8:43-48), Matthew (9:20-22) and the Gospel of Mark (5:25-34) there are descriptions of the story of a woman who had been bleeding for years. I included all three because they provide a more complete picture of what occurred.

Luke 8:43-48
And there was a woman who had had a discharge of blood for twelve years, and though she had spent all her living on physicians, she could not be healed by anyone. She came up behind him and touched the fringe of his garment, and immediately her discharge of blood ceased. And Jesus said, "Who was it that touched me?" When all denied it, Peter said, "Master, the crowds surround you and are pressing in on you!" But Jesus said, "Someone touched me, for I perceive that power has gone out from me." And when the woman saw that she was not hidden, she came trembling, and falling down before him declared in the presence of all the people why she had touched him, and how she had been immediately healed. And he said to her, "Daughter, your faith has made you well; go in peace."

Matthew 9:20-22
And behold, a woman who had suffered from a discharge of blood for twelve years came up behind him and touched the fringe of his garment, for she said to herself, "If I only touch his garment, I will be made well." Jesus turned, and seeing her he said, "Take heart, daughter; your faith has made you well." And instantly the woman was made well.

Mark 5:22-24
And there was a woman who had had a discharge of blood for twelve years, and who had suffered much under many physicians, and had spent all that she had, and was no better

but rather grew worse. She had heard the reports about Jesus and came up behind him in the crowd and touched his garment. For she said, "If I touch even his garments, I will be made well." And immediately the flow of blood dried up, and she felt in her body that she was healed of her disease. And Jesus, perceiving in himself that power had gone out from him, immediately turned about in the crowd and said, "Who touched my garments?" And his disciples said to him, "You see the crowd pressing around you, and yet you say, 'Who touched me?'" And he looked around to see who had done it. But the woman, knowing what had happened to her, came in fear and trembling and fell down before him and told him the whole truth. And he said to her, "Daughter, your faith has made you well; go in peace and be healed of your disease."

From Scripture, we are told that this woman had spent all her money on trying to find a cure for a disease that has plagued her for twelve years. She was bleeding and thus was considered unclean according to Levitical law. If a woman was bleeding for any reason, she was not to take part in worship or other ceremonies. In the passage from Luke, we are told that she was no longer hidden, and she came up behind him (also in the other two passages). She touched the fringe of his garment- which, according to Pulpit Commentary[103] for Deuteronomy 22:12 were the four tassels on the cloak of a Hebrew man to separate himself from unbelievers, to serve as a reminder for Israel to keep the commandments and be set apart as holy unto the Lord. For anyone to grab a hold of a tassel would have been unthinkable. For anyone to grab any part of a male's clothing would have been unthinkable!

---

[103] http://biblehub.com/commentaries/pulpit/deuteronomy/22.htm

I am reminded of the very conspicuous dress of Arab men. I could not imagine a stranger, much less a female stranger approaching any man in public today to grab a hold of an unrelated man's garment. If a woman dared to do that in a country like Saudi Arabia, she would be at once imprisoned! Even in more relaxed religious countries like those of Southeast Asia, this would not be a good practice and the family members of the woman attempting to do that would try to restrain her, while the public would cast derision on her and say she was of loose morals.

The tassels on the Jewish man's tunic were not just an ordinary piece of adornment - this was the part of the man's clothes that set him apart for the Lord (Numbers 15:38). So, it seems that Jesus was also wearing the clothing that was common to Jewish men during that time period. The bleeding woman must have used every ounce of the faith she had, for she was trembling (Luke and Mark passages) and then realized the gravity of who she touched, for she immediately fell down before him and declared the truth. One of the commentaries states that the Greek term she used was "I shall be saved" (instead of "I shall be made well") and in the Greek terms, Jesus replied with "Go in peace and be *whole.*"

Did Jesus scold her for grabbing him in public among a throng of people? No.

He simply turned around and asked her a question to see what she would confess to him. She told him all that happened to her and "declared in the presence of all the people why she had touched him and how she had been immediately healed." Not only did Jesus heal her, He made her whole – wholly restored to the community, whole as a person, and whole in the Kingdom of God as one of His adopted children. His response to her confession can be summed up in one word for me: **Daughter.**

In the earlier chapters, I mentioned the separation women have from Allah in prohibition to prayer when they are bleeding, for they are unclean. Women in the Middle East don't talk openly about bleeding, especially in relation to prayer and Allah. They deal with it by themselves and some never come to an understanding of why these rules of being clean and unclean (haram or haraam) exist. There are many rules that exist for bleeding women that both Muslim men and women may not understand either. When I have shared about this my own testimony, both Muslim men and women seem to want to argue that exceptions exist in Islam. Here are rulings from clerics from an Islamic website:[104]

1 – Prayer (formal prayers) including reciting the Quran out loud.
2 – Fasting –It is haraam for a menstruating woman to fast, ... she has to make up any obligatory fasts that she misses...
3 & 4– Tawaaf around the Ka'bah (pilgrimage)
5 – Staying in the mosque. It is haraam for the menstruating woman to stay in the mosque and even in the Eid prayer-place.
6 – Intercourse It is haraam for her husband to have intercourse with her, and it is haraam for her to allow him to do so
7 – Divorce - It is haraam for a husband to divorce a menstruating woman during her menses [al-Talaaq 65:1]

[104] https://islamqa.info/en/answers/70438/rulings-on-menstruation

8 – Reckoning the 'iddah of divorce by means of the menstrual cycle "And divorced women shall wait (as regards their marriage) for three menstrual periods" [al-Baqarah 2:228]

My first encounter with the Biblical account of the Bleeding Woman was as a brand-new believer. I had not yet heard fully read all the miracles my Savior had done. As a new believer, I was told to read the Gospel of John to understand Christ. After I read the Gospel of John, I decided to start at the beginning of the New Testament. I found this amazing passage in the Gospel of Matthew. Just being presented with the three short verses, the love of Jesus and tenderness in the word "daughter" made me come undone. I sobbed uncontrollably on the floor because it recalled my struggle in prayer as a Muslim woman who was trying to add good works to her scales of judgment -- only to fall short from bleeding every month during my period and so much more after childbirth. Added to that grief was my parents and family who disowned me when I accepted Jesus as my Lord and Savior. *I had no one to call me "daughter," except for the Lord of the Universe.*

What an unimaginable realization of the love of God it was for me to see that two thousand years ago, Jesus of Nazareth thought that women were worthy enough to not just be a part of the amazing miracles he performed, but that he would reach down, pick them up and restore them lovingly to himself. When the world turned their faces away from them, labelled them unworthy and unclean - he called them *"daughter."*

## *The Adulterous Woman*

John 8:6-11

"...but Jesus went to the Mount of Olives. Early in the morning
he came again to the temple. All the people came to him, and
he sat down and taught them. The scribes and the Pharisees
brought a woman who had been caught in adultery and placing
her in the midst they said to him, "Teacher, this woman has
been caught in the act of adultery. Now in the Law, Moses
commanded us to stone such women. So what do you say?"
This they said to test him, that they might have some charge to
bring against him.
Jesus bent down and wrote with his finger on the ground. And
as they continued to ask him, he stood up and said to them,
"Let him who is without sin among you be the first to throw a
stone at her." And once more he bent down and wrote on the
ground. But when they heard it, they went away one by one,
beginning with the older ones, and Jesus was left alone with
the woman standing before him. Jesus stood up and said to
her, "Woman, where are they? Has no one condemned you?"
She said, "No one, Lord." And Jesus said, "Neither do I
condemn you; go, and from now on sin no more."

A woman who had been caught in adultery should have been
severely punished by stoning according to Levitical law was
brought in front of Jesus by the leaders. As a Rabbi (teacher of
Jewish law), he would have known and understood what they
wanted. Instead, Jesus shows mercy and care to the woman,
while showing the men who had gathered around them their own
spiritual state. Was Jesus approving her adultery? No, he
recognized it as sin and he demonstrated his judgment on all who
were in his presence. Romans 3:22-23 states "And this
righteousness from God comes through faith in Jesus Christ to all
who believe. There is no distinction, for all have sinned and fall
short of the glory of God." The Old Testament says in Jeremiah

17:13, "Lord, hope of Israel, those who leave you will be shamed. People who quit following the Lord will be like a name written in the dust, because they have left the Lord, the spring of living water." We do not know what the Lord was writing in the dust of the ground. However, we do know that his presence, tone, demeanor of his person caused all to stop, think and quietly leave. The mob's anger dissipated at his words and the presence of the Prince of Peace prevailed.

In contrast to this mercy shown by Christ is an incident that occurred in 1986 with the stoning of Soraya Manutchehri in the village of Kuhpayeh, Iran. Her husband wanted to marry a 14-year-old girl and keep the dowry money he received when he married Soraya, so he made up false charges of adultery which are punishable by death in Islam. The story gained momentum in 2009 when a movie was made based on the French-Iranian journalist Freidoune Sahebjam's (1933-2008) book published in 1990 titled "La Femme Lapidée." It should be noted that while the Quran does not explicitly state that stoning is the remedy for adultery but does prescribe lashing, there are several Hadith that beg the question and state that death is allowable as a punishment, while other Hadith mention stoning.
An online website called "The Religion of Peace" has an exhaustive list of the Hadith, as well as other references.[105] Even

---

[105] Stoning and Adultery. The Religion of Peace Website. Retrieved online https://www.thereligionofpeace.com/pages/quran/adultery-stoning.aspx

though Muslims around the world publicly stated that stoning was not sanctioned anymore in Muslim countries, in 2014, a couple was arrested in Iran for merely writing a review on the movie and what their thoughts were about stoning for adultery.[106] Other cases have received coverage in the media since then of stoning for adultery, including a vicious case in Somalia of Aisha Ibrahim Duhulow who was 13 years old and was raped in 2008.[107] Amnesty International and other agencies cried for justice for the child who was stoned by 50 men in front of an audience of 1000, while those who raped her suffered no penalties. Amnesty International also has published data gathered in Syria where women have been killed in the same way between 2012 and 2015.[108]

Christianity forbids adultery but it likewise forbids other sexual sins. There is no corporate punishment ascribed to men or women in the New Testament. Rather, there is a call towards church discipline and a request for repentance for sins committed. The theme is right behavior, repentance and restoration with the Lord and with the church community. In the Bible, there is the consistent reminder to go and sin no more.

---

[106] Iranian writer given long jail term for story about stoning Retrieved online https://www.bbc.com/news/world-middle-east-37575193
[107] Somalia: Girl stoned was a child of 13. Amnesty International Website. Retrieved online https://www.amnesty.org.uk/press-releases/somalia-girl-stoned-was-child-13
[108] Syria: Torture was my punishment. 5 July 2016. https://www.amnesty.org/en/documents/mde24/4227/2016/en/

## The Woman healed on the Sabbath

In the Gospel of Luke 13:10-17, there is an account of a woman who suffered from a disability and was healed by Jesus.

"Now he was teaching in one of the synagogues on the Sabbath. And behold, there was a woman who had had a disabling spirit for eighteen years. She was bent over and could not fully straighten herself. When Jesus saw her, he called her over and said to her, "Woman, you are freed from your disability." And he laid his hands on her, and immediately she was made straight, and she glorified God. But the ruler of the synagogue, indignant because Jesus had healed on the Sabbath, said to the people, "There are six days in which work ought to be done. Come on those days and be healed, and not on the Sabbath day." Then the Lord answered him, "You hypocrites! Does not each of you on the Sabbath untie his ox or his donkey from the manger and lead it away to water it? And ought not this woman, a daughter of Abraham whom Satan bound for eighteen years, be loosed from this bond on the Sabbath day?" As he said these things, all his adversaries were put to shame, and all the people rejoiced at all the glorious things that were done by him."

This story is only noted in Luke and not in the other Gospel accounts. It may be due to Luke's experience as a physician that this miraculous healing captured his attention, for he wrote the details of the disease and the number of years she suffered. Here, Jesus is noted as teaching in a synagogue on a holy day of worship. Even though the woman was crippled, she managed to come to worship the Lord. As soon as Jesus saw her, he touched and healed her completely. Her response was what we all should do – to glorify God. However, seeing the miracle did not satisfy those who were watching, including the ruler of the synagogue.

The Bible says that the ruler of the synagogue was "indignant." The Merriam Webster dictionary defines the word as "feeling or showing anger because of something unjust or unworthy." The hypocrisy in the synagogue ruler's actions contradict his words. He seemed to be irate because work was being done on the Sabbath, which was forbidden in Jewish law but did not. Jesus came to make things new. He came to heal and to set things right.

His reply points to the heart of the person by calling him and the leaders "hypocrites." Hypocrites were Greek actors who wore a mask that showed two faces (tragedy/comedy). Again, Jesus sides with the minority in the Jewish culture. A crippled woman would live in the fringes of society and depend upon relatives or others to help support her every need. Many times, these people today are neglected by society and they find it difficult to find work due to their disability. In freeing the woman from bondage due to illness, Jesus not only healed her physically, but also spiritually and restored her socially. The adversaries were put to shame and all people rejoiced!

### *The Canaanite Woman*

Matthew 15:21-28

"And Jesus went away from there and withdrew to the district of Tyre and Sidon. And behold, a Canaanite woman from that region came out and was crying, "Have mercy on me, O Lord, Son of David; my daughter is severely oppressed by a demon." But he did not answer her a word. And his disciples came and begged him, saying, "Send her away, for she is crying out after us." He answered, "I was sent only to the lost sheep of the house of Israel." But she came and knelt before him, saying, "Lord, help me." And he answered, "It is not right to take the children's bread and throw it to the dogs." She said, "Yes, Lord, yet even the dogs eat the crumbs that fall from their masters' table." Then Jesus answered her, "O woman, great is your faith! Be it done for you as you desire." And her daughter was healed instantly."

The land of Canaan was abhorrent to the Jews since the time of the Old Testament due to their idolatry and pagan practices. According to Biblical scholars, Canaanites practiced child sacrifice and cult prostitution.[109] Jews considered gentiles to be unclean and sometimes referred to them as dogs. The Greek word is "kuon" which means "wild cur" which was not the word Jesus used here to refer to the woman. Without knowing or understanding the context of the words used or the background, it is easy to misunderstand what Jesus says to her.

The website Got Questions says the following about what the verses mean:

> "At this point, Jesus explained His current ministry in a way that both the woman and the watching disciples could understand. At that time, His duty was to the people of Israel, not to the Gentiles (Matthew 15:24). Recklessly taking His attention from Israel, in violation of His mission, would be like a father taking food from his children in order to throw it to their pets (Matthews 15:26). The exact word Jesus used here, in Greek, was kunarion, meaning "small dog" or "pet dog." This is a completely different word from the term kuon, used to refer to unspiritual people or to an "unclean" animal.[110]

---

[109] Dillon, K. The Gospel Coalition Dec. 11, 2014
https://www.thegospelcoalition.org/article/gods-justice-in-the-land-of-canaan/
[110] https://www.gotquestions.org/Canaanite-woman-dog.html

This interpretation of the Gospel account makes sense, since Jesus did not get angry with her, but entered into conversation by telling her that His primary concern and business was that He came for the lost sheep. The woman did not take offense but seemed to understand what He said because of her reply that was made in great submission to His authority as Lord. Her faith in Him was rewarded for He immediately healed her daughter and commended her in front of others – even though she was an unclean gentile who was despised by the Jews around Him. Even the crumbs of grace and mercy that fall off the table of our Lord are satisfying to us who believe in His power.

### The Widow's Son

Luke 7:11-17

"Soon afterward he went to a town called Nain, and his disciples and a great crowd went with him. As he drew near to the gate of the town, behold, a man who had died was being carried out, the only son of his mother, and she was a widow, and a considerable crowd from the town was with her. And when the Lord saw her, he had compassion on her and said to her, "Do not weep." Then he came up and touched the bier, and the bearers stood still. And he said, "Young man, I say to you, arise." And the dead man sat up and began to speak, and Jesus gave him to his mother. Fear seized them all, and they glorified God, saying, "A great prophet has arisen among us!" and "God has visited his people!" And this report about him spread through the whole of Judea and all the surrounding country."

In another miracle of raising the dead to life, Jesus goes into a town with quite an entourage. As they entered into the town of Nain, they were met with a funeral procession and another great

crowd following behind. The funeral was for the only provider
for a widow and in essence, was a double tragedy for now she
would have no one to care for her. The Lord Jesus saw the
woman and had compassion on her. *The Lord saw her.*

In Genesis 16, we are given another instance where the Lord
sees a woman in distress and has great compassion on her. That
woman was Hagar as she was fleeing from Abraham's wife Sarah
(her name was "Sarai" at that time). The tender care the Lord
gave to Hagar (Hajar in Arabic) in the form of a blessing is the
same tender care given here to the widow. Just as a note, Hagar is
revered in Islam, for she is the mother of Ishmael and the well the
Lord provided for her in that passage as she ran is believed by
Arabs to still give water. It is maintained that the well is located
near the Kaaba in Mecca, between the hills of al Safa and al
Marwa.[111] In my testimony book "From Isa to Christ," I
explained this in more detail as it relates to the process of the
annual pilgrimage (Hajj) to Mecca that Muslims run back and
forth between these hills to commemorate Hagar's flight into the
desert. They stop and drink at the well of Zam Zam – at separate
places for men and women.[112] I was told that if you drink from
that well, all your illnesses will be cured. Even though my
parents gave each one of us a drink of water from that well, I still
suffer from migraines.

---

[111] Firestone, R (1992). "Ibrāhīm". Studia Islamica (76): 15–18.
[112] Sabah, M. (2017). From Isa to Christ – A Woman's Search for the Hand of
God. Gethsemane Press.

In the Bible, when Hagar received this miracle from the Lord, she calls Him "El Roi" in Hebrew, it means God who sees me. "So she called the name of the LORD who spoke to her, "You are a God of seeing," for she said, "Truly here I have seen him who looks after me." (Genesis 16:13). God not only saw her but also cared for her in time of great need.

Just as the Lord gave Hagar a son (Ishmael) to take care of her in the Old Testament, so did Jesus bring the widow's son back to life from the dead in the New Testament. He ordered the young man to arise. It's curious to read the wording of the Bible, for it says, "And the dead man sat up and began to speak…" Dead people don't sit up or speak, yet we see that one touch from the Lord Jesus Christ and the dead man sat up and spoke. This is the miracle of Christ. He brings dead people to life through the power of His Holy Spirit and the words of the Gospel. Our response for that gift of new eternal life should be to rise up and speak praises of His glory daily! Our Lord has power over death and life – this is the good news of the Gospel. We also know that when Jesus returns on judgment day, He will call forth all dead out of their graves to give a reckoning. This thought should cause all believers to have a fear of God, but not to be afraid of Him. 1 John 4:13-18 states:

"By this we know that we abide in him and he in us, because he has given us of his Spirit. And we have seen and testify that the Father has sent his Son to be the Savior of the world. Whoever confesses that Jesus is the Son of God, God abides in him, and he in God. So we have come to know and to believe the love that God has for us. God is love, and whoever abides in love abides in God, and God abides in him. By this is love perfected with us, so that we may have confidence for the day of judgment, because as he is, so also are we in this world. There is no fear in love, but perfect love casts out fear. For fear has to do with punishment, and whoever fears has not been perfected in love."

May we look forward to that day of resurrection because of the love and confidence we have in our Lord's finished work on the cross.

## Mary Magdalene

John 20:1-18

"Now on the first day of the week Mary Magdalene came to the tomb early, while it was still dark, and saw that the stone had been taken away from the tomb. So she ran and went to Simon Peter and the other disciple, the one whom Jesus loved, and said to them, "They have taken the Lord out of the tomb, and we do not know where they have laid him."

So Peter went out with the other disciple, and they were going toward the tomb. Both of them were running together, but the other disciple outran Peter and reached the tomb first. And stooping to look in, he saw the linen cloths lying there, but he did not go in. Then Simon Peter came, following him, and went into the tomb. He saw the linen cloths lying there, and the face cloth, which had been on Jesus' head, not lying with the linen cloths but folded up in a place by itself. Then the other disciple, who had reached the tomb first, also went in, and he saw and believed; for as yet they did not understand the Scripture, that he must rise from the dead. Then the disciples went back to their homes.

But Mary stood weeping outside the tomb, and as she wept, she stooped to look into the tomb. And she saw two angels in white, sitting where the body of Jesus had lain, one at the head and one at the feet. They said to her, "Woman, why are you weeping?" She said to them, "They have taken away my Lord, and I do not know where they have laid him." Having said this, she turned around and saw Jesus standing, but she did not know that it was Jesus. Jesus said to her, "Woman, why are you weeping? Whom are you seeking?" Supposing him to be

the gardener, she said to him, "Sir, if you have carried him
away, tell me where you have laid him, and I will take him
away." Jesus said to her, "Mary." She turned and said to him in
Aramaic, "Rabboni!" (which means Teacher). Jesus said to her,
"Do not cling to me, for I have not yet ascended to the Father;
but go to my brothers and say to them, 'I am ascending to my
Father and your Father, to my God and your God.'" Mary
Magdalene went and announced to the disciples, "I have seen
the Lord"—and that he had said these things to her."

Mary Magdalene was a Galilean woman who most likely took
her name from the town of Magdala, located on the west bank of
the Sea of Galilee. Jesus delivered her from seven demons,  as
reported in the Gospel of Luke 8:2 and Mark 16:9. She became a
follower of Jesus (Matt. 27:57), a witness to the crucifixion and
burial (Matt. 27:61; 28:1; Mark 15:40, 47; John 19:25), and was
among the women who went to the tomb on Sunday (Mark 16:1
and John 20:1).

The great distinction Jesus also gave her was that she was the
first person to see Jesus alive (Mark 16:9) and was the first one to
tell the other disciples (Luke 24:10; John 20:18) of the Lord's
resurrection. She came to the tomb with other women to finish
the burial process of anointing the body with herbs and spices as
was custom in Judaism. She had been one of the very few at the
foot of the cross and had seen the torture of the crucifixion. Since
it was fresh in her mind, she stood there at the tomb, weeping for
her Lord.

At first, she did not recognize the risen Christ. She assumed
he was the gardener. When she heard her Shepherd's voice call
out her name, she immediately knew who was the One who

called her. John 10:2-3 states Jesus's own words "But he who enters by the door is the shepherd of the sheep. To him the gatekeeper opens. The sheep hear his voice, and he calls his own sheep by name and leads them out." She heard His voice and threw herself upon his feet in love and adoration, for He said "Do not cling to me…" There was something He wanted her to do for the kingdom and that was to be the first one to proclaim the good news of the Gospel – Jesus Christ has risen from the dead. With joy, with haste and with zeal, she went and did exactly that. She testified, "I have seen the Lord" and told them what He had said to her.

Whenever I share my testimony about the Lord Jesus Christ, I have this passage in my mind. I want to be like Mary at the tomb who races back to declare the news of victory in Christ that "I have seen the Lord!" I pray to speak about the testimony He gave me in a clear manner with conviction about facts of His life and resurrection. I pray that this is my life's work and the main thing I am remembered for when I am gone to be at home with my Savior.

What a great honor Christ gave to a mere woman. He took someone whose life had been terrorized by demons and He made her the first evangelist by commissioning her to speak the words of His triumph over the grave and the fulfillment of His promise in Matthew 16:21 that He would suffer, be crucified and in three days, He shall rise again from the dead.

### Eve in the Bible

As in the discussion of the women in Islam, Eve is central to the discussion about Christianity. While Jesus did not directly have interactions with Eve in the Gospels or New Testament, she is nevertheless important for the purpose of this book. Eve was the second human being to be created. The Bible gives great detail and spends time discussing how Eve was brought into being. She was to be a "helper" for Adam and was created by God. Genesis 2: 18-23 states:

> "Then the LORD God said, "It is not good that the man should be alone; I will make him a helper fit for him." Now out of the ground the LORD God had formed every beast of the field and every bird of the heavens and brought them to the man to see what he would call them. And whatever the man called every living creature, that was its name. The man gave names to all livestock and to the birds of the heavens and to every beast of the field. But for Adam there was not found a helper fit for him. So the LORD God caused a deep sleep to fall upon the man, and while he slept took one of his ribs and closed up its place with flesh. And the rib that the LORD God had taken from the man he made into a woman and brought her to the man. Then the man said,
> "This at last is bone of my bones
> and flesh of my flesh;
> she shall be called Woman,
> because she was taken out of Man."
> Therefore, a man shall leave his father and his mother and hold fast to his wife, and they shall become one flesh. And the man and his wife were both naked and were not ashamed."

From Strong's commentary, the Hebrew[113] word for bone is *"etsem"* and has the dual meaning of "self" or "selfsame,"

---

[113]Strong's Hebrew: 6106. עֶצֶם (etsem)
https://biblehub.com/hebrew/strongs_6106.htm

indicating that Adam held this woman as the same as himself and reiterated that by saying "and flesh of my flesh." As Adam spent time with God, giving names to the animals and their mates, he realized there was no creature suitable for him. God in His great providence creates (in His own image- Genesis 1:27) a helpmate for Adam. She was his as he was hers and they knew no shame.

In Genesis 3, Then, the serpent lied to Eve "But the serpent said to the woman, 'You will not surely die. For God knows that when you eat of it your eyes will be opened, and you will be like God, knowing good and evil.' So when the woman saw that the tree was good for food, and that it was a delight to the eyes, and that the tree was to be desired to make one wise she took of its fruit and ate, and she also gave some to her husband who was with her, and he ate" (Genesis 3:4-7). The passage here clearly states that Eve disobeyed God first. However, it might be interesting to note that while Adam squarely placed the blame upon Eve, Christianity does not. The Bible places the blame on Adam in Romans 5:19 "For as by the one man's disobedience the many were made sinners, so by the one man's obedience the many will be made righteous." An article by Dr. Georgia Purdom on the website Answering Genesis[114] explains this:

"From these verses and others in Genesis 1–3 it is clear that the husband was created to be the leader in the marital relationship and that the wife was created to be the helper

[114] Purdom, G. May 29, 2012 "Who Gets the Blame for Original Sin – Adam or Eve?" https://answersingenesis.org/sin/original-sin/who-gets-the-blame-for-original-sin/

(Genesis 2:18). As the leader it was Adam's responsibility to protect and provide for his family. This leadership role was clearly demonstrated when God talked with Adam and Eve following their sin. Even though Eve sinned before Adam, God questioned Adam first (Genesis 3:9). This was because of the leadership role God ordained for husbands in marriage. Adam, as the leader of the family, was held responsible, not only for his own sin of eating from the tree, but also because he did not provide adequate protection for his wife, allowing her to sin.
In the New Testament, Adam is clearly presented as both progenitor and representative of all mankind. The following passages state that Adam is the person through whom sin and resulting death entered the world: For since by man came death, by Man also came the resurrection of the dead. For as in Adam all die, even so in Christ all shall be made alive. And so it is written, "The first man Adam became a living being." The last Adam became a life-giving spirit. (1 Corinthians 15:21–22, 45). Therefore, just as through one man sin entered the world, and death through sin, and thus death spread to all men, because all sinned…
For if by the one man's offense death reigned through the one, much more those who receive abundance of grace and of the gift of righteousness will reign in life through the One, Jesus Christ. Therefore, as through one man's offense judgment came to all men, resulting in condemnation, even so through one Man's righteous act the free gift came to all men, resulting in justification of life. For as by one man's disobedience many were made sinners, so also by one Man's obedience many will be made righteous. (Romans 5:12, 15, 17–19)."

Even though Eve was disobedient to God first, the promise of reconciliation with God was also given to her. Genesis 3:15 says that the seed (singular) would come and crush the enemy's head. Galatians 3:16 tells us that seed is Jesus Christ, the Savior. God prepared the way for a Savior for the human race before the world came to be.

It is important to note that in contrast, Islam blames Eve and then extends that blame to all women henceforth. In addition, there is no redemption or fixing the situation, since Islam does not have a narrative on how death entered the world. Adam and Eve sinned, and Allah forgave them. The story ends there for Muslims. If you sin, that's your own fault and you need to pay Allah back for that through good works.

For Christians, however, the story began in the Garden of Eden, for through woman would come the promised Messiah and Genesis 3:15 marks that promise made by God to humanity for redemption and making all things right. There was a plan from the start. The account also goes on to say that while God provided a plan, there was still punishment for disobedience for both Adam and Eve in the next two verses. However, the verse in Genesis 3:21 showed me the heart of God "And the LORD God made for Adam and for his wife garments of skins and clothed them." Adam and Eve were ashamed, and they had covered themselves with leaves from the Garden. In this verse, we see that God Himself killed the animals He had created and then made clothing for them both.

I taught my children that while God was sad about how Adam and Eve disobeyed Him, He still took care of His creation. He took time to lovingly sew something for each one to wear so they wouldn't get cold. The Lord gives us all we need and provides for those needs with things that are not perishable – thus He meets both out physical and spiritual needs.

As a woman, Eve was treated the same as Adam. She was punished for her transgression against God. The difference here is that the Bible does not blame all women or call them evil for what Eve did, instead both were cast out together and had to deal with the consequences of their actions. The New Testament opens with the birth of the Savior and brings to fruition God's promised. He delivered a Savior named Jesus the Messiah, the sinless lamb of God.

# Chapter 8

# Explaining the Gospel to Muslims

Our salvation story begins and ends in the Garden. As Christians, we ought to understand that Adam and Eve sinned against God and that action resulted in death entering the world. The creation account in the Holy Scriptures has been a point of contention not only from the Muslims but also from atheists and other unbelievers. The website Answering Genesis presents this important connection:

> "The Apostle Paul inseparably connects Jesus to Adam. Jesus came to rectify the damage done by Adam (Romans 5:12–19; 1 Corinthians 15:21–22 and 1 Corinthians 15:45). Adam brought sin and death into the world; Jesus brought righteousness and life into the world. The good news of the gospel cannot be properly understood without understanding the bad news of Genesis 3. We are all sinners in need of a

Savior because we inherited our sin nature from Adam and
have rebelled against God just as he did.
No Adam: no gospel. If Adam and the Fall are not historical,
then Jesus died for a mythological problem and He is a
mythological savior offering us a mythological hope.[115]"

In the mainstream view of relativism, there seem to be a growing
cultural idea that all roads lead to heaven. The Quran teaches that
a Muslim's good works will get them into Paradise. But they
have no idea what each of those works weigh on the great scale
of Allah on judgment day. This is the problem I had with Islam. I
was trying to do good works, but at the end of the day, I was not
sure if my good works were enough, for I was sinning daily.
The Quran says:

"To those who believe and do deeds of righteousness hath
Allah promised forgiveness and a great reward" (Surah 5:9).
"O you who believe! If you are careful of (your duty to) Allah,
He will grant you a distinction and do away with your evils and
forgive you; and Allah is the Lord of mighty grace," (8:29,
online, trans. by M.H. Shakir).
"Then those whose balance (of good deeds) is heavy, they will
be successful. But those whose balance is light, will be those
who have lost their souls; in hell will they abide," (23:102-103).
"And We set a just balance for the Day of Resurrection so that
no soul is wronged in aught. Though it be of the weight of a
grain of mustard seed, We bring it. And We suffice for
reckoners," (21:47).
"They are those who deny the Signs of their Lord and the fact
of their having to meet Him (in the Hereafter): vain will be their
works, nor shall We, on the Day of Judgment, give them any
weight." (18:105)

---

[115] Mortenson, Dr. T. In Defense of the Historical Adam (2015). Retrieved
online https://answersingenesis.org/bible-characters/adam-and-eve/defense-of-
historical-adam/

The Quran teaches that there is a great reward for those who do two things: 1. Believe in Allah and 2. Do deeds of righteousness. If the balance on the judgment scale ends up lighter than you thought, in hell you will abide. Allah will judge and he will determine what the weight is and how vain their works were. On that final day, there will be no "Savior" because you are responsible for your own way to Paradise.

There is a tremendous amount of uncertainty for the Muslim! Heaven is not guaranteed and for women, the odds are even worse, for Muhammad himself was reported in the Hadith saying "Narrated 'Imran bin Husain: The Prophet said, "I looked at Paradise and found poor people forming the majority of its inhabitants; and I looked at Hell and saw that the majority of its inhabitants were women.[116]"

> Narrated by al-Bukhari, Vol.1, Book 6, 301 and Vol. 3, Book 48, 826[117]

> "It was narrated that Abu Sa'eed al-Khudri (may Allah be pleased with him) said: "The Messenger of Allah (peace and blessings of Allah be upon him) went out to the musalla (prayer place) on the day of Eid al-Adha or Eid al-Fitr. He passed by the women and said, 'O women! Give charity, for I have seen that you form the majority of the people of Hell.' They asked, 'Why is that, O Messenger of Allah?' He replied, 'You curse frequently and are ungrateful to your husbands. I have not seen anyone more deficient in intelligence and religious commitment than you. A cautious sensible man could

---

[116] Sahih al-Bukhari, Book 54 of Beginning of Creation, Hadith 464 retrieved online https://muflihun.com/bukhari/54/464
[117] Sahih al-Bukhari, Book 6 of Menstrual Periods, Hadith 301 retrieved online https://muflihun.com/bukhari/6/301 and https://muflihun.com/bukhari/48/826

be led astray by some of you.' The women asked, 'O Messenger of Allah, what is deficient in our intelligence and religious commitment?' He said, 'Is not the testimony of two women equal to the testimony of one man?' They said, 'Yes.' He said, 'This is the deficiency in her intelligence. Is it not true that a woman can neither pray nor fast during her menses?' The women said, 'Yes.' He said, 'This is the deficiency in her religious commitment.'"

When someone online asked a question why women in hell outnumbered the men, the answer from Islam Q A was the following (emphasis mine):

"Our believing sisters who learn of this hadeeth should behave like those Sahabiyat (female Companions) who, when they learned of this, did good deeds which would be the means, by Allah's leave, of keeping them far away from being included in that majority of the inhabitants of Hell.

So our advice to the sisters is to strive to adhere to the rituals and obligatory duties of Islam, especially prayer, and to keep away from that which Allah has forbidden, especially shirk in **its many forms which is widespread among women, such as seeking one's needs from someone other than Allah, going to practitioners of witchcraft and fortune-tellers, etc.**

We ask Allah to keep us and all our brothers and sisters far away from the Fire and the words and deeds that bring one close to it."[118]

In other words, "Best of luck to you. Hope you will make it." These are the very words I heard on the day of my grandmother's funeral "Inshallah [Arabic: If Allah wills it]. Hope she made it." My immediate thought upon hearing that exchange was "What if she didn't make it? What if I don't make it? How do I know?"

---

[118] Munajjid, S. More Women in Hell Than Men? retrieved online https://islamqa.info/en/answers/21457/more-women-in-hell-than-men

The answer to that is that a Muslim doesn't know until after they die. There is no telling if Allah will accept or change his mind – for Muslims believe that he can change his mind and can deceive others. One of Allah's names in the Quran is "**al Makr**" in Surah Ali Imran 3:54 which translates to "**deceiver.**" There are several Arabic and Muslim websites that confirm this translation. The website Islam Quest[119] explains it in this way:

"The meaning of "Makr": The literal meaning of "Makr" is devising and planning. It can be good or evil [1] as well as it being capable for being for good or for evil. However, some believe "Makr" to mean tricking and when attributed to Allah, to refer to the punishment of tricking and deception.[2] The "Makr of Allah": When examining the verses in which the word "Makr" has been used,[3] we realize that the meaning of "Makr" is simply devising and planning and that it could be good or evil. For example in the verse "[4],و يمكرون و يكمر الله والله خير الماكرين" the word "يَمْكُرُونَ" refers to the plotting of the Mushrikin (Pagans) that intended to kill the prophet or imprison him and the phrase "يَمْكُرُ اللَّهُ" refers to Allah's devising and commanding the prophet to immigrate. The very fact that the word "مكر" is used along with the adjective "السَّيِّئَى" (evil) in the Quran [5] proves that "Makr" can be good or evil. Therefore, the many verses that attribute Makr to Allah refer to his supreme regulation and management of matters, because He is the true owner of all devising and there is no devising separate from his.

As a result, Allah has supremacy over all planners [6], and the verse from Surah Ra'd[7] clearly states that Allah is the supreme deviser and that the plotting of others is nothing compared to His.[8]

[1] Qurashi, Seyyed Ali Akbar, Qamuse Quran, vol. 6, pg. 265.
[2] Al-Munjid, translation, Muhammad Bandar Riki, vol. 2, pg. 1820.
[3] A'raf:99 and 123; Fater:10 and 43; Ra'd:33 and 42; Saba':33; Yunus:21; Ale Imran:54; Nahl:26 and 45; Naml:50 and 51; Nuh:22; Ibrahim:46; Yusuf:13; Ghafir:45.

[119]What is meant by Makr of Allah that has been mentioned in the Quran? Retrieved online https://www.islamquest.net/en/archive/question/fa297

[4] Anfal:30.   [5] Fater:43.   [6] Ale Imran:54.   [7] Ra'd:42.[8] Tabatabai, Seyyed Muhammad Husein, Al-Mizan, Farsi translation, Musavi Hamedani, vol. 12, pg. 355, 20 volume version, Entesharate Eslami Publications.

Even Muhammad's trusted companion and father of Aisha (his wife), Abu Bakr was reported as saying, "By Allah! I would not feel safe from the deception (Makr) of Allah, even if I had one foot in paradise."[120] If Abu Bakr (who is greatly esteemed in Islam) was not sure if he was going to make it, what hope does an average Muslim have of gaining Paradise?

These were the concerns I had as a Muslim early on in my teenage years. I was unsure of where I was going, and that uncertainty manifested into a growing despair as an adult woman. I was never sure if I was working enough to gain Allah's favor and, in the meantime, I lied, cheated and did bad works. I compare it to the national debt – I did not feel like I could make the scales of Allah balance out or tip in my favor on judgment day. So, what is the hope for anyone who thinks they can get to heaven on the basis of their own merit?

### *The hope is in Christ alone.*

John 1:17 says "For the Law was given through Moses; grace and truth came through Jesus Christ." In John 14:1-6 Jesus speaks of going to Heaven to prepare a place for us. He also affirms that He is the way, the truth and the life.

[120] Khalid Muhammad Khalid "The Successors of the Messenger" translated into English by Muhammad Mahdi Al-Sharif. p.70.

"Let not your hearts be troubled. Believe in God; believe also in me. In my Father's house are many rooms. If it were not so, would I have told you that I go to prepare a place for you? And if I go and prepare a place for you, I will come again and will take you to myself, that where I am you may be also. And you know the way to where I am going." Thomas said to him, "Lord, we do not know where you are going. How can we know the way?" Jesus said to him, "I am the way, and the truth, and the life. No one comes to the Father except through me."

In the Bible, Satan is called the "Father of lies" (John 8:44) and a "deceiver" (Revelation 12:9). We believe that the Holy Scriptures contain the truth of God as revealed by the Word of God, Jesus. In an exchange with Pontius Pilate, before his crucifixion, John 18:37 reports "Then Pilate said to him, "So you are a king?" Jesus answered, "You say that I am a king. For this purpose I was born and for this purpose I have come into the world—to bear witness to the truth. Everyone who is of the truth listens to my voice."

God is truth and in Him there is no darkness or change. James 1:17 attests to this "Every good gift and every perfect gift is from above, coming down from the Father of lights, with whom there is no variation or shadow due to change" as well as 1 John 15 "This is the message we have heard from him and proclaim to you, that God is light, and in him is no darkness at all." God does not change or deceive anyone. He is light and life. He is holy.

There was great comfort for me when I read the following words after my conversion to Christianity:

"In the beginning was the Word, and the Word was with God, and the Word was God. He was in the beginning with God. All things were made through him, and without him was not anything made that was made. In him was life, and the life was the light of men. The light shines in the darkness, and the darkness has not overcome it. (John 1:1-5)."

The ultimate sin in Islam is called "shirk" which is placing someone or something equivalent to Allah and the literal translation from the Quran is "ascribing a partner to Allah." They blame Christians for the unforgivable sin of shirk and there are articles and videos online that tell Muslims that Isa never claimed to be God. This is why accepting Jesus Christ as Lord and Savior is of ultimate importance. Islam's central creed, the Shahada rejects this as does daily prayer performed five times a day. There is a Hadith that states:

"Abu Zubair reported: Ibn Zubair uttered at the end of every prayer after pronouncing salutation (these words): **"There is no god but Allah. He is alone. There is no partner with Him.** Sovereignty belongs to Him and He is Potent over everything. There is no might or power except with Allah. There is no god but Allah and we do not worship but Him alone. To Him belong all bounties, to Him belongs all Grace, and to Him is worthy praise accorded. There is no god but Allah, to Whom we are sincere in devotion, even though the unbelievers should disapprove it." (The narrator said): He (the Holy Prophet) uttered it at the end of every (obligatory) prayer.[121]"

Surah Al An'am 6:101-102
[He is] Originator of the heavens and the earth. **How could He have a son** when He does not have a companion and He created all things? And He is, of all things, Knowing. That is Allah, your Lord; there is no deity except Him, the Creator of all things, so worship Him. And He is Disposer of all things.

[121] Sahih Muslim, Vol. 2, Book of Prayers, Hadith 1235 Retrieved online https://muflihun.com/muslim/4

Daily, Muslims reject the fact that Jesus is God incarnate and they deny the trinity. This is ingrained in the teachings and practice of Islam.

The Quran itself calls Isa Ibn Maryam "Kalimat Allah" or literally translated to "Word of Allah" in Surah an Nisa 4:171. The verse in 1 Peter 2:22 (noted on the next page) states Jesus had no sin. In Surah Ali Imran 3:45-55, the Quran states that Isa Masih is the word of Allah, is the Messiah, is the only sinless man, is righteous, is given wisdom, giver of life [to clay birds through his breath], cures the blind, the leper, and gives life to the dead (3:49). As if that was not enough, the Quran in Surah al Zukhruf 43:61 says Isa Masih will come back to judge on judgment day. In order to explain this verse, there is an important Hadith:

"Narrated Abu Huraira: Allah's Apostle said, "By Him in Whose Hands my soul is, surely (Jesus,) the son of Mary will soon descend amongst you and will judge mankind justly (as a Just Ruler), he will break the Cross and kill the pigs and there will be no Jizya (i.e. taxation taken from non-Muslims). Money will be in abundance so that nobody will accept it, and a single prostration to Allah (in prayer) will be better than the whole world and whatever is in it." Abu Huraira added "If you wish, you can recite (this verse of the Holy Book): -- 'And there is none of the people of the Scriptures (Jews and Christians) But must believe in him (i.e Jesus as an Apostle of Allah and a human being) Before his death. And on the Day of Judgment

He will be a witness Against them." (4.159) (See Fateh Al Bari, Page 302 Vol 7).[122]"

As a Muslim, I had known about Isa coming back on judgment day and when I read more about this prophet Isa Masih in the Quran, I could not reconcile the differences between him and other prophets, including Muhammad—the differences in the way of life, the miracles and the way of his death. All these things differed from the other prophets. The Quran offers no escape from Allah's judgment. It presents confusing information that is incomplete, so there has to be an explanation given in the Hadith (and even then, it makes no sense sometimes, like why would Isa break the cross and kill the pigs in the passage above?). There is no way for a Muslim to be secure that they have a place in Paradise. As mentioned before, the odds are stacked more heavily against women.

This passage in 1 Peter 2:21- 25 sums up the Gospel:

"For to this you have been called, because Christ also suffered for you, leaving you an example, so that you might follow in his steps. He committed no sin, neither was deceit found in his mouth. When he was reviled, he did not revile in return; when he suffered, he did not threaten, but continued entrusting himself to him who judges justly. He himself bore our sins in his body on the tree, that we might die to sin and live to righteousness. By his wounds you have been healed. For you were straying like sheep but have now returned to the Shepherd and Overseer of your souls."

[122] Sahih al-Bukhari, Book 4 of Prophets, Hadith 657 retrieved online https://muflihun.com/bukhari/55/657

Before we do anything to connect with Muslims, we ought to pray for the Lord to open the minds and make ready the hearts of Muslims so they will hear the words of Christ through the power of the Holy Spirit. Only the Holy Spirit can bring the dead to life through the miraculous words of the Gospel.

# Chapter 9

# Hospitality – The Invitation

Hospitality is a recurring theme in my life, especially growing up in the Middle East and Pakistan. In fact, I could not imagine my life without friends, family and yes, unknown people I have brought home for a hot cup of tea. It was happening so often that my children would often come home and wonder why there wasn't an unknown car in the driveway because they were so used to meeting new women sitting at the kitchen table.

My life has been enriched by most of these encounters (yes, some of them were downright weird, but that's just expected!). My notion of hospitality does not come from having a perfect home (which I do not.), a perfectly appointed kitchen (my kitchen is very nice, but not perfect in the least), a perfect family (I think we all know that our families are less than perfect!), or a perfect life. In fact, I have been known to have dishes in the sink, stuff on the counter, and groceries still in the bag when I've had people over... why? Because that's just life.

So, why all this talk about hospitality?

If you're a Christian, you don't have to have a special spiritual gift for it (that's just an excuse) and the early Christians practiced hospitality years after Christ's death and resurrection. Those who are believers in Christ are distinctly commanded to show such hospitality (see 1 Timothy 3:2; Titus 1:7-8; Romans 12:13; Hebrews 11:13). One of my favorite passages in the Bible is when Abraham welcomed strangers to rest after their long journey (Genesis 18:2-8). In Deuteronomy, the act of sharing food (Deuteronomy 14:28-29) to help others is emphasized as a blessing. The early church made it a habit to gather together to break bread as a new family in Christ and praise God (Acts 2:42-47). A beautiful gift of hospitality was given to Jesus Christ by Zacchaeus. Out of the joy he had in meeting Christ, salvation came to his house that day (Luke 19:5-6)! What a gift he received in turn from our Lord and Savior!

We miss out on blessings to give and receive when we cordon off a part of our lives to others. The early Christians wanted to be a part of one another's life because many had their own families disown them for following Jesus. This was my own experience when the Lord called me to leave Islam and become a Christian. If others had not invited me into their homes, what family would I have had? I was blessed because several women in that church came forward and told me that they would be a grandmother to my children and a mother to me. Others reminded me that they were there to help with my young children and that we should never feel alone.

Jesus redefined the family while He was suffering on the cross. "When Jesus saw his mother and the disciple whom he loved standing nearby, he said to his mother, "Woman, behold, your son!" Then he said to the disciple, "Behold, your mother!" And from that hour the disciple took her to his own home."" John 19:26-27. Even when in excruciating pain, Jesus made sure His disciples were not abandoned. He took care to let them know that they were a part of His spiritual family and that they would never be forsaken.

I praise God that He invites us to His table to partake His daily bread – so then why can we be so stingy and miserly in the way we invite others? What grace you have been given in Christ? It's time to go out there and share the love of Jesus, the Gospel through an invitation into your home and witness the way the Holy Spirit uses these everyday things to bring salvation to their house!

Those from the East are used to visiting homes of friends and family. Some of my earliest memories are of celebrating Eid in Saudi Arabia. We would put on our best clothes, grab sweets and small presents and go from house to house, celebrating with friends. The same traditions continued when I moved to Pakistan and to the United Arab Emirates. People were always coming and going from our home. It was a very warm and welcoming place. My mother, an impeccable hostess, always had hot tea, delicious snacks and beautiful china ready to go in case someone happened to drop by.

When we moved to the United States, however, these visits were far less frequent. Many Pakistanis came to our home from our community, but we did not receive many invitations to dine at American people's homes. This experience is shared by others who are foreigners or even are people of another ethnicity who live here. When I bring up the Eastern culture of hospitality to people, many look at me wistfully and then tell me that stopping by a friend's home for a cup of tea went away in the 1950's. It is old-fashioned and just not done anymore – kind of like writing in cursive or posting a hand-written letter through the post office.

At my family's home, there is a long-standing tradition of tea time at 4:00 pm. This is something I have held onto all my life. Even today, my friends know that around 4:00 pm, there I will be sitting at my kitchen table, drinking a cup of tea. I also know that around the same time daily, I can find my parents doing the same thing across the United States. It's a tradition and it is so soothing – like a cool oasis in the middle of the desert.

Even when I worked full time, I would stop what I was doing and make a quick cup of tea around 4:00 pm. My co-workers began to join me at my desk in this tradition because nearly everyone experiences a mid-day slump around that time. It made the rest of the day go by exceedingly fast.

A cup of hot tea has a wonderful soothing property to it. There is nothing like making a little pause in the day to stop everything and just take a small breather to drink tea. It is a refined tradition and one I love to pass on to my friends. I have had the chance to make real friendships, make a connection and share my home with many. Some of these people I have known for a long time. Others may be people I have just met once or twice.

People are generally surprised at the offer of coming over to my home for a spot of tea. I am met usually with a smile of surprise. It is much more common to get together at a fancy coffee shop or any other place. Hospitality, along with slowing down to enjoy a cup of tea has also gone by the wayside. When I ask women why that is the case, many tell me that they feel pressure to have their home "just right" or even "perfect." With three children and a hectic schedule, I found myself wondering when that day would come! I don't think we have had our home looking "just right" since the day we moved in. If I waited around for that very day, I shudder to think of all the beautiful conversations, the tears of sorrow and pain, the joy of new friendships and renewing of old friends I would have missed over the years.

I had the opportunity a few years ago to see a former Muslim author speak about cultural expectations. He shared a very poignant example about how a foreign exchange student came from the Middle East with two suitcases – one had his personal items and clothes, the other was full of beautifully wrapped gifts. When asked if he had family or friends here that he was bringing the gifts for, the student replied that he didn't know anyone in the United States, but when he was invited to their home, he wanted to bring a gift as is customary in that culture. The worst part of this story was that the student returned home to Saudi Arabia with one suitcase still packed full of the wrapped packages, for no one had invited him.

At home, near our kitchen table, I have a reminder verse that he Lord gave me this place to bring others into my life "And day by day, attending the temple together and breaking bread in their homes, they received their food with glad and generous hearts… Acts 2:46." So many Christians close off their homes to others, citing one reason after another. Even though we have entertained many people in our home, an invitation in return to come to other people's homes is still sparse. Is it an indication of some who are uncomfortable to see their personal life and living spaces – to not be able to "come as you are" or literally show our dirty laundry? Or is it a sign of being connected via social media but not in face to face gatherings? I think this may be one of the reasons why so many Millennials say that they feel lonely and have no close friends.

When you come to my home, you might see my daughter's books around the fireplace in our living room. Sometimes, there may be a pile of freshly washed laundry being sorted on the living room couch. My craft tools might be scattered about on the kitchen island and there definitely will be yarn on the couch where I sit in the evenings to knit or crochet. It's not a perfect home, but then neither am I a perfect human being. I see this as a sort of ministry (yes, to have a messy home – not dirty, but messy!). I have had women tell me that seeing my house as it is makes them want to invite someone over and not have that pressure to have it looking like a model home.

If we keep wearing masks, we can inadvertently cast aside endless opportunities. There is something authentic about people seeing your home with a messy counter. There is something genuine about reaching across the table and sharing a plate of cookies with a steaming cup of hot tea. The Bible teaches Christians to open their homes as a sacrificial way to love others. It is such a simple way to promote unity in the Church and sets a wonderful foundation to build relationships for Evangelism.

In the ancient times, there were numerous wars fought with thousands of soldiers upon the battlefield. There were those who carried the banners, those who recorded the battle as historians and those who were tasked with one job - to be a runner. These soldiers would travel long arduous distances by foot to tell the kingdom of the success of the battle. The watchmen would be on the lookout to spot these bearers of the good news that said, "Victory is Ours!" The runners were called "Evangelists" or literally, "those who bring good news." from Greek *eu-* **good** plus *angelos* **messenger**. So, the term existed before

Christianity[123] but the New Testament uses ***euangelion***
considerably to denote the Good News of the Resurrection of
Christ. The battle has been won, death has been defeated by
Christ and we are freed by His work on the cross. Our job as
Christians is to bring a message of the good news of Jesus to
others. How do we do this in our everyday lives?

Over the year, I have seen complicated presentations of
Evangelism and even programs built around how to evangelize to
others. When I teach classes about Islam or share my testimony, I
inadvertently get asked about how to reach out to Muslims. It
might seem very simple, but I recommend just saying "hello!"
with a genuine smile. Ask about their family or children. These
are things you would normally do with someone else – why
should Muslims be any different? The answer is that there is a
mindset and sometimes a physical barrier created by a hijab. I
urge you to not let someone's clothing get in the way! I
sometimes dress in my Pakistani clothes for functions and can
end up at the grocery store or running errands wearing them. I am
a Christian who is dressed in that way – you never know who you
might end up meeting.

Early in my walk with Christ, some people told me that there
was a special prayer that others had to recite to receive Christ or a
special tract to use to convert others. To me, Evangelism is

---

123

http://www.perseus.tufts.edu/hopper/wordfreq?lang=greek&lookup=eu%29ag
ge%2Flion

shared life and sharing the life-giving words of the Gospel. It is welcoming a stranger into the home, into the family, into the Christian community and into the walk with Christ. It is not treating people (including Muslims) as a special project. In essence, it is the invitation before the invitation to follow Christ or to be discipled. It is having the genuine desire to be friends, to be inconvenienced when someone needs a ride to the airport or wants to meet you at dinnertime on a Sunday. It can be messy, problematic and disruptive to our regular lives. Yet, it is one of the most rewarding things we can be a part of – to share in God's ministry and to bring the light of Jesus into the lives of others.

These interactions create a desire to know one another as friends and then to have them ask about the hope we have in Jesus (1 Peter 3:15). That is where we need to share the life-giving words of the Gospel to point back to Jesus so that others may see Him and not our works. Our own testimony is bearing witness to what Jesus has done for us – however, that is not the Gospel. The Gospel is purely focused on Jesus Christ and the singular work He did on our behalf upon the cross. Apart from that, you are sharing a good story about your own life! My life changed when I heard about what Jesus did for me – that He came down and lived a life of perfect submission to God, that He was crucified as an atonement for my sins, that He rose again from the dead so I could have access to God the Father through His Spirit (Ephesians 2:18). When I heard these glorious truths, I couldn't wait to tell others about what I heard!

May we be like the early church and share our home with others. May we be a mother, sister, daughter or friend to those who have no one to depend upon. May we have open hearts, open doors and open invitations to others. May we comfort others as God comforts us.

# Chapter 10

# Counting the Cost

I met Halima through a Christian friend who thought it would be good for me to get to know her, and to speak with her about Islam and Christianity. I had the opportunity to share the Gospel with her fairly early on in our friendship and after a couple of years of meeting together, I decided one day to give her a Bible. She had many questions at each one of our meetings and was eager to learn more about Jesus. When I handed her the Bible as a gift, she was reluctant to take it. She said that it might not be a good idea for her to have a Bible at home, since her husband might find it offensive. I told her that it was up to her to decide but that it was the best gift I could ever give to another person, for it contained the words of God Almighty and the answers to many things she had asked me over the years. You see, Halima knew that the simple act of taking a Bible home meant that she might have to pay dearly for that decision. She was counting the cost.

There is a reason Jesus tells us to count the cost of becoming a disciple. Here in the United States, people can freely attend church. If they don't like the church they are attending, they simply go to the next one down the street and continue until they find one that fits their needs. The American church is looked upon as something that exists for consumption by the worshipper, complete with programs that are designed to entertain babies, children, youth and adults – not as a place to worship and focus on the One true God. I have had several friends tell me that they were "church shopping" to find one that fit their children's programming needs and developmental needs. No mention of spiritual peace, prayer, or worship. As an Easterner, I do not understand this. I also cannot comprehend where this notion comes from as it's not in the Bible or presented anywhere by Jesus to have His body, the church function as a customizable program to fit one's personal desires, moods or preferences.

Church was established in the book of Acts as the *ekklesia* (Greek - ones called out).[124] "The "called-out assembly," then, is a congregation of believers whom God has called out of the world as Romans 8:28 states "And we know that for those who

---

[124] What is the definition of ekklesia? Got Questions Website. Retrieved online https://www.gotquestions.org/definition-ekklesia.html

love God all things work together for good, for those who are
called according to his purpose" and "into His wonderful light"
(1 Peter 2:9)." Those called out by God from darkness should
look remarkably different than the world around them. I am not
saying that Christians should be arrogant or have a "holier than
thou" attitude. I am saying that there is a problem when you
cannot tell the difference between a follower of Jesus and a
follower and a follower of worldly things.

The cliché Christian slogans posted on church road signs or
T-shirts seem to affirm the culture and trying to present Jesus in a
casual and fun way to the public. In a book "The Holiness of
God" by American author and theologian R. C. Sproul, chapter
one opens with the prophet Isaiah who has a vision of the throne
room of God (Isaiah 6). As soon as he catches a glimpse of His
majesty and glory, he falls to his face and says, "Woe is me, I am
a man of unclean lips!"

That's *not* what the average American church-goer seems to
experience. In church, I don't normally see people falling down
in awe to worship the majesty of God nor give Him the honor
that He deserves. Instead, I see a casual attitude (casual clothes
are one thing, it's the attitude I'm talking about) that bleeds over
into a casual approach of Christianity and a cavalier handling of
the Holy Bible – if the Bible is being read at all. I don't think
many think of following Christ being associated with having a
cost in this society or repentance for sinning against a holy God.

Again, R.C. Sproul (1985) reminded us that:

"The idea of holiness is so central to biblical teaching that it is said of God, "Holy is his name" (Luke 1:49). His name is holy because He is holy. He is not always treated with holy reverence. His name is tramped through the dirt of this world. It functions as a curse word, a platform for the obscene. That the world has little respect for God is vividly seen by the way the world regards His name. No honor. No reverence. No awe before Him."[125]

Before I became a follower of Jesus, I had a profound respect for Jesus as one of Allah's important prophets. I would have never thought to use his name as an exclamation or use it in any way that would bring shame upon Allah, Islam or any of the prophets. When I became a Christian, I did not see this respect shown by others. While there were some who regarded Jesus as who He is – the second person of the Trinity, fully equal to God the Father. However, much to my distress, there were the majority who did not seem to have any notion of reverence. I was surprised one morning at church when I saw a woman bring her cup of coffee and donut into the sanctuary. As a new Christian, I had learned that when Christians entered into the sanctuary to worship, they were supposed to be in the presence of God Himself. I would never think to bring in my coffee cup to come into a meeting with a CEO for work, much less bring it in to worship the maker of the heavens and the earth. Muslims seeing this would not understand either. They have strict rules and procedures before setting foot into a mosque and they understand

[125] Sproul, R.C. (1985). The Holiness of God (1st Tyndale House Publishers ed.). Carol Stream, IL: Tyndale House Publishers.

structure, formality and preparation for prayer in a place of worship. One normally doesn't find a box of donuts in the main worship area or even in a gathering area of a mosque.

Where has the reverence gone? Has it taken a back seat because of trying to please the culture and taking a secular approach to Jesus to make His teachings more palatable? Is it because there is a tremendous focus at Christmas time on Santa rather than on Christ? Is it because we think about his humble birth as a baby and less (if not at all) about the price he paid on the cross for the remission of our sins? Should we continue to watch as friends, family and other Christians continue to behave in ways contrary to Scripture without remorse? I believe this stems from not knowing who we worship and not reading the Bible to find out who God is through His revealed word.

We can start reaching out to the world if we start holding one another accountable and have the church look different than the culture. Let's stop conforming to the standards of the world and be transformed by the renewing of our mind (Romans 12:2). We are all sinful, that's true -- but we should still be working out our salvation with fear and trembling (Philippians 2:12) and not have a laid-back attitude about things that might cause others to stumble. Sproul (1985) further stated in his book:

> "The simplistic way of not conforming is to see what is in style in our culture and then do the opposite. If short hair is in vogue, the nonconformist wears long hair. If going to the movies is popular, then Christians avoid movies as "worldly." The extreme case of this may be seen in groups that refuse to wear

buttons or use electricity because such things, too, are worldly. A superficial style of nonconformity is the classical Pharisaical trap. The kingdom of God is not about buttons, movies, or dancing.
The concern of God is not focused on what we eat or what we drink. The call of nonconformity is a call to a deeper level of righteousness, that goes beyond externals. When piety is defined exclusively in terms of externals, the whole point of the apostle's teaching has been lost. Somehow, we have failed to hear Jesus' words that it is not what goes into a person's mouth that defiles a person, but what comes out of that mouth. We still want to make the kingdom a matter of eating and drinking."

— R.C. Sproul, The Holiness of God

In the Gospel accounts, there were many who came to hear Jesus. There were crowds of thousands who loved to hear Him preach, to tell about the love of God the Father and to even hear about the blessings (Beatitudes). There were others who came to be healed, to see miracles be performed and to be fed from the overflowing loaves and fishes. There were still others who came because they were curious and were jealous, like the Pharisees and they were waiting to catch Jesus in the act of violating some rule or Roman law. When suffering came, at the foot of cross on Calvary's hill, there were only a handful of followers. All those big crowds had disappeared because many thought that Jesus's teachings were too hard (John 6:60). Jesus defined what it meant to be a disciple when He still had great crowds around Him.

"Now great crowds accompanied him, and he turned and said to them, 'If anyone comes to me
and does not hate his own father and mother and wife and children and brothers and sisters, yes, and even his own life, he cannot be my disciple. Whoever does not bear his own

cross and come after me cannot be my disciple. For which of you, desiring to build a tower, does not first sit down and count the cost, whether he has enough to complete it? Otherwise, when he has laid a foundation and is not able to finish, all who see it begin to mock him, saying, 'This man began to build and was not able to finish.' Or what king, going out to encounter another king in war, will not sit down first and deliberate whether he is able with ten thousand to meet him who comes against him with twenty thousand? And if not, while the other is yet a great way off, he sends a delegation and asks for terms of peace. So therefore, any one of you who does not renounce all that he has cannot be my disciple (Luke 14:25-33)."

The truth of the Gospel message is that to follow Christ, you must die to your old ways, your old self, your traditions and beliefs. Jesus calls us out of our family, out of homes, out of our comfort zone, and out of our current lifestyle. These may not be common experiences one has when becoming a believer in Christ in the United States. In fact, Christians in the West sometimes don't think about or want to think about the cost or suffering. Jesus says "renounce" in the last sentence of the verse above. The Cambridge[126] dictionary online defines the term as "to say publicly that you no longer own, support, believe in, or have a connection with something." There are some who like the idea of Jesus (His peace, forgiveness, teaching) but don't want to change how they live their life or give up the views they hold (abortion, alcohol, sex, etc.). Jesus says, "So therefore if any one of you who does not renounce all that he has cannot be my disciple."

The early church understood these things when they were persecuted by their families and were forced out of their homes

---

[126] https://dictionary.cambridge.org/us/dictionary/english/renounce

and cities. Facing great trials, they were flogged, publicly stoned and fed to the lions in the Circus Maximus during Nero's reign. They paid for following Jesus with their lives, yet to the death each proclaimed Him as Lord and Savior. There are former Muslims around the world who are facing these realities today – all for following Jesus. Ones who commit to follow Jesus are not aiming to find happiness in their lives but to live in the shadow of the only one who could give them eternal life – even at the risk of suffering great punishments.

In Islamic communities, Muslims count their good deeds and bad deeds daily. Some even say they are earning "heavenly currency" through their good works and are busy using Apps for their phone to track these deeds! All are told up front what monumental costs they will have to pay if they turn away from their religion by being called an apostate or a Kafir. They can be disowned by their family, friends, community even here in the United States. In Muslim countries they can lose their jobs, and also their life. In the Quran (2:217), an apostate (one who has turned their back to Islam and converted to another religion) has the penalty of death on their head for men. For women, it is life imprisonment. The website Al Islam[127] clearly states this reality:

> "The punishment prescribed by the shari`ah for apostasy is death. Even the terms used by the shari`ah for apostates give the idea of treason to this whole phenomenon...

---

[127] https://www.al-islam.org/articles/apostacy-islam-sayyid-muhammad-rizvi

In the first case, the apostasy is like the treason against God; whereas in the second case, the apostasy is like the treason against the Muslim community."

Women in Islam definitely have additional costs that they have to bear. Their husbands could divorce them and take away their children and the whole community would turn their backs on them. I have known women here in the United States who had to face that reality. They could be cut off financially from any means – the church needs to be able to help disciple the new believer and let them know honestly what lies ahead of them but also to reassure them that their church family can help in so many ways! Some of the Muslims I have known were beaten, punished or sent back to their home country. This is not just an outcome for women. I have also known this to be true for former Muslim men who have declared Christ as Savior. For Jesus said also in the Gospel of John 15:20 "Remember the word that I said to you: 'A servant is not greater than his master.' If they persecuted me, they will also persecute you. If they kept my word, they will also keep yours."

The cost to follow Christ affects believers wherever we are-- in the United States, Middle East or anywhere else in the world. The difference is that for a Muslim to turn her back on might be the same as signing a death warrant since there are clear guidelines in Islam. Jesus warns us about that as well "For whoever would save his life will lose it, but whoever loses his life for my sake and the gospel's will save it (Mark 8:35)." When the gift of eternal life is given, it is offered at the time of conversion. This fact was what I held on to tightly when I converted to Christianity and my family disowned me. My cost was not that I had to renounce all I knew – Christ had already told me what my cost was to be, which was rejection, derision and separation. I lost my place in the community I grew up in – my aunts, uncles, family friends, and the people I knew since I moved to the United States did not want to have anything to do with me. I was not invited to their homes. They knew I was a Christian and a Kafir – they were not to be friends with me. For others in Muslim communities, it could be loss of a job, clientele or schooling for their children. In Pakistan, Christians are segregated out into their own small communities where everyone knows their location and address, thus they are regularly denied jobs or opportunities. The great exchange for me, however was the peace of Christ in my life and home, the love of God the Father and the gift of eternal life that can never be taken away from me.

Are Christians ready to look at the Church as it was designed to be? A place of awe and reverence for the Almighty God? A place where the Word of God is preached, and lives are changed daily through the Word to help us resemble the likeness of Christ? A sanctuary of hope for those who follow Christ and serve others out of the overflow of thanksgiving for what Jesus has done for them and not as something that exists for their own consumption? Is the Church ready to be the family of Christ for

Muslims who lose their family? Are we truly open to accepting someone to live with us in our home if they were cast out of theirs? Are we willing to watch their children if they have no income and need to find a job to pay bills and keep food on the table? Are we willing to give if they have left their home with nothing other than the clothes on their back? Think about these things and then consider what the cost is to follow Jesus for a Muslim. They can lose all this and more. They can lose their life, but they will gain it for the sake of the kingdom.

*Just as Jesus promised.*

# Chapter II

# Made Whole in Jesus

*For this reason I bow my knees before the Father, from whom every family in heaven and on earth is named, that according to the riches of his glory he may grant you to be strengthened with power through his Spirit in your inner being, so that Christ may dwell in your hearts through faith—that you, being rooted and grounded in love, may have strength to comprehend with all the saints what is the breadth and length and height and depth, and to know the love of Christ that surpasses knowledge, that you may be filled with all the fullness of God.*

*Ephesians 3:14-19*

Since I have shared bits and pieces of my testimony and conversion in this book and more completely in the book "From Isa to Christ – A Muslim Woman's Search for the Hand of God," I wanted to share what it means to be made whole in Christ. The Bible contains a lot of information of what a life in Christ should look like, but it is not a manual or a checklist. Rather, being in Christ is a way of life. Conversion is being born again, where you die to your old self, the Holy Spirit gives us new birth (1 Corinthians 5:17) and we are raised to walk in the newness of life (Romans 6:4). When explaining being born again, Jesus said these words to Nicodemus, a Pharisee and ruler of the Jews:

> "Jesus answered him, "Truly, truly, I say to you, unless one is born again, he cannot see the kingdom of God." Nicodemus said to him, "How can a man be born when he is old? Can he enter a second time into his mother's womb and be born?" Jesus answered, "Truly, truly, I say to you, unless one is born of water and the Spirit, he cannot enter the kingdom of God. That which is born of the flesh is flesh, and that which is born of the Spirit is spirit." (John 3:3-6).

In the Old Testament, the book of Ezekiel (36:25-27) gave a preview to the Israelites of what God was going to do through His Christ:

> "Then I will sprinkle clean water on you, and you will be clean; I will cleanse you from all your filthiness and from all your idols. Moreover, I will give you a new heart and put a new spirit within you; and I will remove the heart of stone from your flesh and give you a heart of flesh. I will put My Spirit within you and cause you to walk in My statutes, and you will be careful to observe My ordinances."

None of these things made any sense to me as a brand-new believer who had not read any Scripture (but was born again through the power of the Holy Spirit and the words of the Gospel shared with my husband and I). I couldn't wait to devour all the words God had spoken in the Bible. Someone suggested I begin with the Gospel accounts to learn about Jesus. I did that and much more – I began a journey into reading the entire Bible and attending Bible Study so I could learn as much as I could. I had missed 35 years of Jesus Christ in my life. I had all intention of catching up as fast as I could!

## A New Life in Christ

The different life in Christ was not a change overnight. I wish it was, but the Lord was patient with me. He showed me where lying was not acceptable. He showed me that even though I was hurt by my Muslim family, I had to forgive them, love them, pray for them and to see them through the eyes of Christ. I had to stop looking at my husband for my fulfillment and look to Christ for my every need as a provider. These things were not easy. I had anger towards others and a sense of entitlement, but the Lord again reminded me through His word that He had shown me great forgiveness for my sins – who was I to have an unforgiving heart?

Having been a Muslim for so many years, I had to re-think my views on works and depend upon God's grace and mercy towards me. Even my prayer life was different. In my former life, I was trying to be a better Muslim, to pray five times a day and to do other things that would bring me more points with Allah. I was literally praying "extra credit" prayers in the evening, the longest prayer of the day! As a Christian, I learned that prayer could take different forms, including singing psalms and hymns of praise. I was not limited to time, space or any ritual washings –

that I was made clean by Christ and could approach the throne of grace at any time through Him.

One of the most difficult things for me to learn was to not say the automatic "Inshallah (Arabic: If Allah wills it)" or "Bismillah (Arabic: I start with the name of Allah)" and other sayings so common for Muslims. I also needed to stop saying "By Allah!" for exclamations of swearing by God's name and start revering God's name as holy, not to be said in vain. I learned from a former Muslim who had dedicated his life to following Christ as a Pastor, that all these changes could come in time and that I didn't have to completely erase everything I knew. He wisely assured me that the Holy Spirit would be my guide and would show me what to change and when.

Since God didn't "need" my good works, what was I supposed to do? I learned that as well. The outpouring of thanksgiving for what God has done for us manifests itself in doing good things for others. Not because we must do them in order to get to Heaven, but because those things glorify our Father in Heaven. Not because of obligation but because of love and a grateful heart.

Even reading the Bible was new. There are steps a Muslim must take before even touching the Quran – one can't simply pick it up and flip through it. Muslims are taught to perform a ritual washing (wudhu) so that you can purify yourself, to only touch it with the right hand, to sit in a clean place, to place it on a rack or a pillow, to say verses to start (Tauz and Tasmia), and more. The book itself is revered and I did not realize I was allowed to carry a Bible in my purse (which I started doing), or that I could read it anywhere and anytime without any compulsion. However, some habits die hard. I shrank in horror at church one time because I saw a good friend of ours start to write and highlight verses in her Bible as the Pastor preached. I didn't know you could write in the Holy Bible and it took me almost a decade to be able to do that! It wasn't until I learned that the Word of God was a person and thus, there was no magic in the paper and ink (as some believe about the Quran) of the book. There is such a freedom in Christ that affects every aspect of your life that many Christians take for granted. Prayer and reading the Bible are just small examples.

**Culture is not Lost, Citizenship is Gained**

When I converted, my mother told me that I had been born a Muslim, so it didn't matter that I became a Christian. I am still not sure what that meant. There is nothing in the Quran that says, "once a Muslim, always a Muslim," but Muslims do believe that every human being was created as a Muslim and that they "revert" back to Islam. Islam also teaches that it's every man (or woman) for themselves. Each has to do their own good works to earn credit or that "heavenly currency" to add to their spiritual bank account for the final Day of Judgment. Muslims believe also that each baby is born as a clean slate and their good/bad deeds are accounted the rest of their lives.

That is definitely not how Christianity works. The Christian belief is that all humanity is born into sin. In fact, David says in Psalm 51:3-5:

"For I know my transgressions,
and my sin is ever before me.
Against you, you only, have I sinned
and done what is evil in your sight,
so that you may be justified in your words
and blameless in your judgment.
Behold, I was brought forth in iniquity,
and in sin did my mother conceive me."
We are made right in front of God through Christ who cleanses us with His righteousness that is imputed to us. Only through His blood are we made whole.

In her disappointment, my mother also told me that she saw my conversion as an "exchange of your Allah necklace for a cross necklace." I wore my Allah necklace all the time and had a custom-made small charm that was a gold Quran with the words "Allah" engraved in gold on one side and "Muhammad" on the other. While it was true that I was now wearing a cross necklace, I told my mom that we Christians did not worship the cross but that it was a reminder of the One who saved us through His death and resurrection on the cross. That statement made no sense to her whatsoever because Muslims do not believe Jesus died on the cross. She also told me that she thought my conversion was so I could make better business connections, for the only Muslims she knew who had gone to church were doing that to get ahead in their careers.

Underneath that derision and disbelief from my mother was a fear that I was not only rejecting my family's religion but also our Pakistani culture. The Muslims in Pakistan believe that once someone turns to Christianity, they are to take a new "Anglo" name like John, Paul or Christine. Later in the conversation, she asked me what my new name was going to be – I did not understand why she was asking me that until after I hung up the phone. The truth is that Jesus's invitation includes every tongue, tribe and nation. He does not tell us to leave our culture, upbringing, ethnicity and become vanilla. However, He does tell us that our one and only allegiance belongs to Him alone.

I am still a Pakistani with the same name. I still wear my national dress of shalwar kameez with a dupatta. I still speak the language fluently. I still look the same as before. None of those things were taken away from me. However, I was given a priceless gift! *I was given my new designation as a citizen of Heaven, with all the rights and privileges given to those who are in Christ.* Paul says in his letter to the Ephesians (2:18-19) "For through him we both have access in one Spirit to the Father. So then you are no longer strangers and aliens, but you are fellow citizens with the saints and members of the household of God."

There are so many speculations by the cultural community as to why a Muslim would ever want to risk being demeaned and disowned by their families but also risk death because they have now become something abhorred in Islam – a Kafir. A Kafir is like a dirty word. It's the scum on the bottom of scum and no one ever wants to become one of those. It's the "boogey man" of Islam – kids know about Kafirs and are in terror of them.

As a Muslim, I was burdened by the nagging suspicion question "What if my good works are not good enough?" Added to that was the fact that I could not piece together the information from the Quran about Isa Masih and asked: Why was he given so many miracles and special treatment? Why was he appointed to come back on judgment day? Something was not right, and some information must have been missing. I just did not know that all the pieces of the puzzle would come together through the incredible words of the Gospel message that Jesus Himself is Lord. There was a change that was taking place in the world through the Gospel as it states in 1 Thessalonians 1:4-5:

> "For we know, brothers and sisters loved by God, that he has chosen you, because our gospel came to you not only in word, but also in power and in the Holy Spirit and with full conviction. You know what kind of men we proved to be among you for your sake."

Today, we still witness the power of those words penned centuries ago by the apostle Paul to the churches in Asia. According to the author David Garrison of the book "The Wind in the House of Islam," more Muslims have committed to following the Lord Jesus as their Savior in this century than in all the centuries combined. This phenomenon even caught the attention of Newsweek magazine in an article titled "Why More

Muslims are Turning to Jesus.[128]" As it was with the first century Christians, persecution brings about growth for the Church around the world.

Becoming a Christian did not mean that my life was now organized, happy, carefree and perfect. Instead, it meant that there were factors to consider for me that I had not thought about before. I actually cared about being in my Father's will – even if it meant rejection from others. I had a desire to know the heart of God. I wanted to read His word so I would know more about His purpose and will for my life – even if that meant suffering. Most of all, I was excited to share the good news of the Gospel with others so they could also know what I know.

**Made Whole in Jesus**

There is a marvelous passage in Colossians 2:8-15:

"See to it that no one takes you captive by philosophy and empty deceit, according to human tradition, according to the elemental spirits of the world, and not according to Christ. For in him the whole fullness of deity dwells bodily, and you have been filled in him, who is the head of all rule and authority. In him also you were circumcised with a circumcision made without hands, by putting off the body of the flesh, by the circumcision of Christ, having been buried with him in baptism, in which you were also raised with him through faith in the powerful working of God, who raised him from the dead. And you, who were dead in your trespasses and the uncircumcision of your flesh, God made alive together with him, having forgiven us all our trespasses, by canceling the record of debt that stood against us with its legal demands. This he set aside,

---

[128] Garrison, D. "Why More Muslims are Turning to Jesus." Newsweek. 06-28-2019. https://www.newsweek.com/christianity-islam-turning-jesus-1446327

nailing it to the cross. He disarmed the rulers and authorities
and put them to open shame, by triumphing over them in him.

The first part of these incredible verses state that it is not human
traditions that should take you captive, nor anything that is not of
Christ. The next part says that we have been filled (some versions
say "made complete") by Jesus. He took all our debts and paid
them at the cross. *We do not have to do any works, look to*
*anything else, compare or compete with anyone because we*
*have been made completely whole in Jesus*. God needs nothing.
He is self-sufficient.

When Jesus healed a person in the New Testament, He healed
the whole person – not just the infirmity. Passage after passage
attests to the fact that Jesus came to bring salvation to the whole
person, not just to perform in front of crowds. There are many
false teachers today who perform for others, to make them
believe that they need to have more faith, do better, give more
money to the church, etc., in order to achieve salvation. When
one understands that nothing needs to be added to Christ, one is
truly freed.

When Christ has makes you whole, there is a satisfaction and
a new sense of self that begins to take place of the old. Jesus
restores us – just like He restored the women He met and healed.
He heals us of the wounds the world inflicts. He heals us from
broken relationships and broken hearts. The broken pieces aren't
just glued together – we receive a new heart:

"And I will give them one heart, and a new spirit I will put within them. I will remove the heart of stone from their flesh and give them a heart of flesh, that they may walk in my statutes and keep my rules and obey them. And they shall be my people, and I will be their God" (Ezekiel 11:19-20).

In John 1:16, "For from his fullness we have all received, grace upon grace." The Bible tells us that in Christ, the moment we believe we receive Christ's fullness and are made whole--all things are made new (Revelation 21:5).

I used to be afraid, downright terrified of death-- just as Muhammad was afraid of death. Because of the free gift of grace from God, I now know that death has no sting. Christ has conquered death and that He is there to help me when I am weak. I can look to Christ to help me when I am fearful, when I am despised by those closest to me and when I suffer, for "For because he himself has suffered when tempted, he is able to help those who are being tempted. (Hebrews 2:18)." I did not realize that I was not put on this earth to face these fears alone, but that Christ who has conquered all this is always there to help me, to encourage me, to guide me and to call me His adopted daughter.

He reminds us that "My Father, who has given them to me, is greater than all, and no one is able to snatch them out of the Father's hand. (John 10:29)." He is our Good Shepherd and He laid His life down for His sheep so that none would perish. What a gift of immeasurable riches is given to us who are made whole in Christ Jesus!

**We do not have to do any works, look to anything else, compare or compete with anyone because WE HAVE BEEN MADE COMPLETELY WHOLE IN JESUS.**

**monasabahbooks.com**

# Epilogue

*A Prayer for the Reader:*

*Almighty God, You are the Creator of the heavens and the earth. You know all things, see all things and know our hearts. You created man and woman in Your own image, and you call us by name. You are the Good Shepherd and you watch over us.*

*Lord, I pray for your sheep. I pray that we will hear Your voice and will come running when You call us. I pray that those who are reading this book will be made aware of who You truly are – the way, the truth and the life. I pray that we will be obedient to Your Great Commission. That we may go out in the power of the Holy Spirit and share the good news of the Gospel – that you came, dwelt among us, were crucified for our sins, were dead and buried. After three days, you rose again from the dead and sit on the right hand of God the Father. You are coming back to judge all of mankind.*

*We praise You that we do not have to fear Judgment Day, for You protect Your sheep and cover us with Your blood. Through Christ, we can approach the throne of God boldly. We love You, Lord and may we live to praise You and You alone.*

*In the name of Jesus Christ who saves us. Amen.*

# APPENDIX

## 100 Questions to Consider

These are questions you can use for a Book Club or a discussion on Islam. These questions also can be used as a check to see how much you know about Islam. They are compiled from hundreds of speaking engagements where I've asked attendees to jot down questions that they would like to have answered about Islam.

NOTE: If you are not able to answer these questions using this book, please consider using the book "Reaching Muslims – A Christian's Guide" as a reference.

1.  What does "Islam" mean?
2.  What does "Muslim" mean?
3.  What is the most important teaching of Islam?
4.  What are 5 beliefs of Muslims?
5.  What are the 5 pillars of Faith?
6.  What happens when a Muslim does not follow the 5 pillars?
7.  What is the relationship between Allah and his followers?
8.  How is Allah different than the God of the Bible?
9.  What do Muslims believe about angels?
10. What do Muslims believe about Satan?
11. What are Jinn?
12. What do Muslims believe about how the world was created?
13. What do Muslims believe about how man (Adam) was created?
14. What do Muslims believe about Eve?
15. What is Original Sin?

16. Do Muslims believe in Original Sin? Why or why not?
17. What are the main prophets in the Quran?
18. How do the prophets of the Quran differ from the prophets of the Bible?
19. What do Muslims believe about Muhammad? Who was he?
20. Who was Isa Ibn Maryam?
21. What are the differences between Isa and Jesus of the Bible?
22. What are the differences between Muhammad and Jesus?
23. Why does the Quran talk more about Isa than Muhammad?
24. What do Muslims believe about Mary (mother of Jesus)?
25. How many wives did Muhammad have?
26. Why did he have so many wives when the Quran only allows four?
27. What is the minimum age for a Muslim girl to be married?
28. What was the name and age of Muhammad's youngest wife?
29. What is the Quran?
30. What is a Hadith?
31. What is a Surah?
32. What is the main language for reading the Quran? Why?
33. Why do women pray behind men?
34. What is the purpose of Muslim prayer?
35. How is Muslim prayer different than Christian prayer?
36. How does Allah determine who goes to heaven or hell on the day of Judgment?
37. How does a Muslim know their works on earth were good enough to get them to heaven?
38. What does Islam promise good Muslims in Paradise? For men? For women?
39. What does Christianity say about Judgment Day?
40. What is a Savior?
41. What are Christians being saved from?
42. How does Jesus save?
43. What does heaven look like in the Bible? How is that different than the Quran?
44. What happened to Adam and Eve after they disobeyed Allah in the Quran?
45. Does Adam go to hell for his sin according to Islam?
46. Who are infidels?
47. What is an apostate?
48. Do Muslims believe in the Torah and the Bible?
49. What are the three main documents that make up Islamic teachings?

50. What are Sunni and Shia?
51. Do Muslims agree with the religious clerics?
52. What is Hijab?
53. Do Muslim women have to cover their faces?
54. Why are men allowed to dress any way they want?
55. Are women and men equal in Islam?
56. Are women allowed to speak on important topics of Islam?
57. Were there historical Muslim women who were leaders?
58. What does the Quran say about women?
59. How are Muslim women treated in Muslim countries?
60. How are Muslim women treated in the United States or Europe?
61. Are women allowed to work outside the house in Islam?
62. Is a woman's inheritance the same as a man's in Islam?
63. How many women does it take to equal one man's testimony in court?
64. Are women stoned for adultery?
65. What are the laws for women caught in adultery?
66. What are the laws for men caught in adultery?
67. What did Jesus teach about adultery?
68. Does Islam encourage honor killings? Why or why not?
69. What are Muslim views on domestic violence?
70. Are there any Muslim scholars?
71. What are Muslim views on education for girls and women?
72. Are Muslim women allowed to date like Western women?
73. How do Muslims customarily get married?
74. Is there a dowry for Muslim women?
75. What are Muslim views on marriage?
76. What are the Muslim views on divorce?
77. Can a Muslim man marry more than one woman?
78. Can a Muslim woman marry more than one man?
79. What is Sharia?
80. Do all Muslims follow Sharia?
81. How does Sharia affect American law?
82. What is a fatwa?
83. Why don't Muslims come out against terrorism?
84. What does the Quran say about war?
85. What does the Quran say about peace?
86. What does the Quran say about Jihad?
87. Why are so many Muslim countries in a state of unrest?
88. Is there a conflict between being a Muslim and being an American?

89. What is contributing to the growth of Islam today?
90. What are the things the church should consider for Muslim converts to Christianity?
91. What is the cost for Muslims who become Christians?
92. Are Muslims forbidden to eat certain things? What?
93. Are Muslims forbidden to drink certain things? What?
94. What does "Halal" mean?
95. Since the Old Testament Bible has food laws, why don't Christians still follow them?
96. What is forbidden to Christians to eat or drink?
97. What did Jesus teach about women?
98. How is that different than Islam?
99. What is the status of women in Islam?
100. Who is coming back to judge on Judgment Day, according to the Quran?

# Acknowledgements

My first recognition of gratitude goes to my family. I appreciate each of you so much. I thank my husband for his encouragement and belief that I could get this book done, especially as I grappled with the 500+ pages of Sharia law, the Sira biography, and other books on my nightstand. I'm grateful for his half-asleep interest in my late-night "random facts about Islam" updates and for not dismissing my phone text updates on my word count status.

Thank you, Sarah for being the greatest cover designer ever! You have an expert eye for color and placement, along with a sense of what is contemporary. I praise God for our son Joshua's quick mind and for coming up with an incredible title that perfectly summed up my whole book. How impressed was I that it took you just a few seconds, while I struggled with a title for at least a year and a half!

I am grateful to my wonderful team of supportive friends and editors who not only encouraged me to write but also provided me with hours of phone call help when I was stuck. This book was not only different in content from my others, but I also wanted to work collaboratively with women to bring it to completion.

A debt of gratitude to Jennifer Boutwell, Tina Koebelin., Laura Igo Young. who not only edited my last book "Reaching Muslims" under pressure and a tight publishing deadline but did so cheerfully! I am so glad you all were up for the task again and were so gracious with your time, skills and brainpower. I praise God that He placed each one of you in my life and gave you such beautiful gifts for sharing with the body of Christ.

A special thank you to Jason Braine who dissected the scripture usage to ensure that I was not inadvertently committing heresy. I rejoice that the Lord has given you the gifts of discernment and wisdom.

Ultimately, I praise the Lord for this book and for giving me the words, the time and energy to write. May it be used to glorify His name in all the world.

*"But, as it is written, "What no eye has seen, nor ear heard, nor the heart of man imagined, what God has prepared for those who love him" ~ 1 Corinthians 2:9*

# About the Author

Mona Sabah was born and raised in the Middle East (Saudi Arabia, Kuwait and United Arab Emirates), went to school in Pakistan and then finally moved to the United States. She speaks English, Spanish, and Urdu fluently. She has worked in the Human Resources field and teaches Leadership and Cultural Diversity. She holds her Master's in Human Resources from the University of San Francisco. She is a professional speaker and a corporate trainer.

Mona was saved from Islam and became a follower of Jesus Christ at the age of 35. Her husband Stephen is the Pastor of Mission Bible Church and they have 3 beautiful children.

She published her testimony "From Isa to Christ: A Muslim Woman's Search for the Hand of God" & a Guide for Christians titled "Reaching Muslims"-both available on Amazon, Kindle and wherever books are sold.

*These books are also presented as a course and seminar. Please contact her if you are interested in bringing it to your area or to schedule her for your next conference.*

**Blog: www.monasabahbooks.com**
**Facebook: @monasabahbooks**
**Church Website: www.mbiblec.com**

*Please consider leaving a book review on Amazon, Google Books and Goodreads. It would be greatly appreciated.

# Also by Mona Sabah

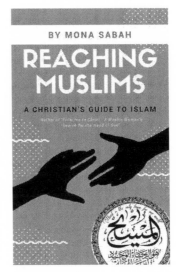

# NOTES

Made in the USA
Middletown, DE
23 December 2019